THE PROPERTY MANAGEMENT HANDBOOK

THE PROPERTY INVESTORS MANAGEMENT HANDBOOK

DAVID WATSON

Emerald Guides
www.emeraldpublishing.co.uk

Emerald Publishing

978-1-84716-544-2

Printed by 4edge Ltd www.4edge.co.uk

Cover design by Bookworks Islington

CONTENTS

****

INTRODUCTION

The aim of this book is to demonstrate in a clear and uncomplicated way the main considerations involved in investing in and managing a residential property portfolio.

Although it is getting harder for the would be landlord to gain access to the buy-to-let sector in the south east of England because of high prices, the opportunities for landlords to invest and make a decent return generally, in particular in the Midlands and North, are better than ever, with rents across Britain set to rise by more than 20% over the next five years in the private rented sector. Overall, private letting of residential property has grown significantly in the last 25 years. However, in some cases those who are involved in letting property do not have the professional knowledge needed to manage effectively and often end up in a mess. Little thought is given to the fact that a complex framework of law covers the landlord and tenant, defining the relationship between the two.

Generally the key to understanding any situation is having knowledge of a particular subject. The law and business environment relating to housing is one very important area.

This book covers the acquisition, letting and managing of property in depth and should enable the landlord, or potential landlord to develop a portfolio of properties and manage effectively and efficiently, at the same time protecting his or her asset, whether it be a house, flat or House in Multi-Occupation.

Also included in this edition is a detailed guide to landlord tax obligations, including capital gains tax and advice on how to minimize liability.

This book is essential reading for any landlord or potential landlord and should prove to be invaluable.

DAVID WATSON

CHAPTER 1

Investing in Property-General Considerations

Investing in Property

The overall demand for private rented property is now stronger than ever, with the mortgage market restricted for purchasers and house price inflation, particularly in the south east, creating the need for high deposits which people cannot find. Lending has become far more stringent, owing to the onset of the credit crunch and the banks unwillingness to loan money, particularly to property investors. Essentially, accessing finance has become a big issue. The banks favor those with large cash deposits. This is the same in the buy-to-let sector as for domestic mortgages.

However, if finance can be arranged then the yields that one can expect from buy-to-let properties are high by comparison, currently standing at 6%. Of course, this depends on where the property is located. See overleaf for a table indicating the best buy to let areas in the UK. A yield is a portfolio's annual rental income as a percentage of total value. The reason is that demand for private rented property is high, particularly as first time buyers cannot get a toehold in the market. They are instead turning to the private rental sector. Therefore, investing in property, for the longer term, as opposed to investing for short-term gain, is still a viable option.

See overleaf-best and worst buy to let areas in the UK.

BUY-TO-LET -RETURN BY AREAS -January 2015

The towns that offer the best buy-to-let returns

Rental returns on buy-to-let are biggest in regional centres like Southampton, Manchester and Nottingham - where one in four homes are now privately rented.

Property investors are looking way beyond London and identifying regions where yields are almost three times as high as in the capital. Cities offering the greatest yields - rental income measured against the property cost - include Southampton, Blackpool, Nottingham and Hull.

The latest data on buy-to-let returns, from lender HSBC, also shows the proportion of property in each area already owned by landlords. And in many of the top-yielding areas private landlords already own one in four properties, or more.

Southampton, with rental yields of 8.73pc, currently tops the list for rental returns. Manchester, Nottingham, Blackpool and Hull complete the top five locations with the best rental yield at 7.98pc, 7.67pc and 7.47pc respectively. In all of those areas, except Hull, private landlords already own one in five properties, or more.

These areas also offer the characteristics that make for excellent buy-to-let investment, the experts say: relatively low house prices coupled with strong demand for rental property from large student and young professional populations.

See overleaf.

Top 10 buy-to-let hot spots by rental yields.

Location	Housing privately rented (%)	Average house price	Average monthly rent	Gross rental yield (%)
Southampton	23.42	£143,011	£1,040	8.73
Manchester	26.85	£104,244	£693	7.98
Nottingham	21.64	£86,000	£550	7.67
Blackpool	24.16	£77,899	£495	7.63
Kingston upon Hull	19.02	£68,243	£425	7.63
Coventry	19.02	£110,029	£650	7.09
Oxford	26.11	£254,514	£1,489	7.02
Portsmouth	22.28	£146,709	£795	6.50
Liverpool	21.75	£91,175	£494	6.50
Cambridge	23.91	£185,414	£1,001	6.48

The lowest yields were registered in areas such as London where recent price rises have been large and rapid, outpacing the growth in rents.

In London in particular, there is a higher proportion of rental property than elsewhere, with 38pc of property in Westminster, for example, being privately rented.

Worst 10 buy-to-let areas by rental yields

Location	Housing privately rented (%)	Average house price	Average monthly rent	Gross rental yield (%)
Kensington and Chelsea	33.97	£1,236,605	£2,968	2.88
Thanet	21.96	£189,362	£524	3.32

Hastings	27.19	£184,787	£520	3.32	
Haringey	30.33	£425,541	£1,200	3.38	
Westminster	37.56	£890,272	£2,578	3.47	
Hammersmith and Fulham	30.05	£685,797	£2,004	3.51	
Richmond upon Thames	20.55	£540,379	£1,699	3.77	
Camden	30.46	£715,831	£2,383	3.99	
Ipswich	18.75	£158,925	£546	4.12	
Lincoln	19.36	£124,789	£433	4.16	

Rental yields

Investment properties which are rented out receive an income from tenants. In order to calculate the gross rental yield the annual rental income is divided by the purchase price of the property (annual rent÷price) X 100 = Gross rental yield)

So, if the property was purchased for £75,000 (total) and the rent received is £450 per month the yield would be:

£5400 (annual rent) ÷ £75,000 X 100 which equals an annual yield of 7.2. This is a very respectable return on your capital. Of course if you are a landlord then you will want to factor in the costs of being a landlord, such as maintenance, insurance, loan costs, empty periods etc.

Capital yields

If and when a property increases with time, this is known as capital growth. A simple example is if you buy a property for £75,000 and it increases by 25% there will be a capital appreciation of £18,750. It is a rule of thumb that low price properties might produce a high rental yield and low capital growth and vice-versa, although this is not always the case.

Again, each case differs and many factors will play a part but as long as you know what you want then you should be safe with your investment.

If you are interested in averages, landlords receive £678 in rent each month as a national average. However, as always, averages don't give the whole picture. Landlords in London and the South East collect the highest rents, with £1,079 and £816 respectively. In the west Midland rents average £678 and in East Anglia £676. Approximately 60% of this is spent on borrowing and management costs, leaving landlords with a healthy 40% profit on average. With buy-to-let mortgage rates so cheap (at the moment) now is the time to expand your portfolio releasing equity and raising deposits to buy new properties. However, when expanding your portfolio it is important to be realistic and ensure that you invest in properties that can be sold on easily, as there may come a time when you need to get your hands on the capital that you have tied up.

As with everything, property is a good investment as long as it is managed well. Too many would-be landlords buy property and neglect it which has a negative impact on the environment and also a negative impact on the investment as a whole. A run down property will decrease in value and the possibility of renting it out for a full market rent will also diminish. That is what this book is all about-how to become a good landlord and a good property manager and how to maximize the returns on your property.

What kind of property is suitable for letting?

Obviously there are a number of different markets when it comes to people who rent. There are those who are less affluent, young and single, in need of a sharing situation, but more likely to require more intensive management than older more mature (perhaps professional) people who can afford a higher rent but require more for their money. The type of property you have, its location, its condition, will very much determine the rent levels that you can charge and the clients that you will attract.

The type of rent that a landlord might expect to achieve will be around ten per cent of the value of the freehold of the property, (or long leasehold in the case of flats). The eventual profit will be determined by the level of any existing mortgage and other outgoings.

If you are renting a flat it could be that it is in a mansion block or other flatted block and the service charge will need to be added to the rent. When letting a property it is necessary to consider profit after mortgage payments and likely tax bill plus other outgoings such as insurance and agents fees (if any). Of course there are other factors which make the profit achieved less important, that is the capital growth of the property. See further on in the book for a breakdown of taxation and allowances.

The importance of having a clear business plan

As a (would be) private landlord, a person considering letting a property for profit, or already doing so, it is vital that you are very clear about the following:

- What kind of approach do you intend to take as a landlord? Do you intend to purchase, or do you have, an up market property which you are going to rent out to stable professional tenants who will pay their rent on time and look after the property (hopefully!).
- What are the key factors that affect the value of a property in rental terms? Is the property close to public transport, does it have a garden, what floor is it on and what size are the rooms? Is it secure and in a crime free area? If you are acquiring a property you should set out what it is you are trying to achieve in the longer term, i.e. the type of person you want and match this to the likely residential requirements of that hypothetical person. You can then gain an idea of what type of property you are looking for, in what area, and you can then see whether or not you can afford such a property. If not, you may have to change your plan.
- Do you intend to let to young single people, perhaps students, who will

occupy individual rooms achieving higher returns but causing potentially greater headaches? Are you aware of the headaches? It is vitally important that you understand the ramifications of letting to different client groups and the potential problems in the future.

- Are you clear about the impact on the environment, and to other people, that your activities as a landlord may have? For example, do you have a maintenance plan which ensures that not only does your property look nice and remain well maintained but also takes into account whether the plan, or lack of it, will have an impact on the rest of the neighborhood? Will the type of tenant you intend to attract affect the rest of those living in the immediate vicinity
- What are the aims and objectives underpinning your business plan? Do you have a business plan or are you operating in an unstructured way? Taking into account the above, it is obviously necessary that you have a clear picture of the business environment that you intend to operate in, the legal and economic framework that governs and regulates the environment.
- It is vital that you are very clear about what it is you are trying to achieve. You should either understand the type of property that you already own or have an idea of the property you are trying to acquire to fit what client group. These goals should be very clear in your own mind and based on a long-term projection, underpinned by knowledge of the law and economics of letting property.
- As an exercise you should sit down and map out your business plan, before you go any further. Whether you are an existing property owner, or wish to acquire a property for the purpose of letting, the first objective is to formulate a business plan.

Now read the main points from chapter one overleaf.

Main points from chapter one

- Letting residential property for investment has become more and more common and has replaced owner occupation as the main form of tenure as people struggle to get on the property ladder.
- The demand for private rented property is set to increase along with an increase in rents.
- There are a number of different markets when it comes to people who rent. The markets are defined mainly by economic factors.
- The type of rent a landlord will expect will vary and the profit will be determined by size of mortgage in relation to rent and also by other outgoings on the property.
- It is vital that a landlord, or prospective landlord has a business plan that sets out aims and objectives of investment.
- It is vital that you are clear about what you are trying to achieve.

****

Chapter 2

The Economics of Developing Your Portfolio

Having looked generally at investment in buy-to-let property, it is now time to consider the actual costs which you will incur when you purchase a property for investment. Your overall budget will consist of finance to buy the property, and costs of acquisition such as stamp duty and conveyancing costs. There may also be the costs of a building survey, ranging from a basic survey to a more in-depth examination. This might lead to extra costs after purchase and before letting.

Your overall budget

Before beginning to look for a house or flat for investment you need to sit down and give careful thought to the overall costs involved in the purchase, which will be in the main mortgage costs, stamp duty and solicitors fees and any refurbishment costs. These are detailed below.

Buy-to-Let Mortgages

Buy-to-let mortgages are slowly becoming more attainable, after a period of retrenchment in the market as a whole, arising because of the banks desire to be cautious in their policies of lending. There is competition now, with Buy-to-let specialist lender Paragon once again becoming active. Typically, a person raising a buy-to- let mortgage will need to find between 25-35% deposit depending on the lender and the deal. First time investors typically need to own their own property to get into the market and also have to demonstrate income of at £25,000 a year.

Lenders also require rents to equal 125% of mortgage payments on a buy-to-let property.

For example, a £500 monthly mortgage repayment would have to achieve rent of at least £625 a month.

Those who already own buy-to-let properties and are looking to expand for the first time since the credit crunch face further hurdles given the lack of finance. It is, however, still very possible to expand a portfolio with several building societies Most mortgage providers allow each investor to have up to 10 properties with a maximum of three mortgaged with that particular lender. It is a case of shopping around for the best deal.

If you are a professional landlord who wants to invest in a larger range of properties you will need to go to a specialist lender. Two such specialist lenders are Shawbrook bank, a recently formed bank and Paragon. They have deals for larger landlords, or those that want to expand, including those with Houses in Multi-Occupation (HMO's).

Currently, at the time of writing in May 2015, the average buy-to-let to year fixed rate is currently 3.6%. the average five year fixed rate is 4.26%. the best deals, as mentioned, are reserved for those with substantial deposits. You will find that the arrangements fees for buy-to-let mortgages become very hefty indeed for those with a lower deposit. For example, Aldemore, who are another specialist lender offers an 80% buy-to-let deal with an arrangement fee of 3%, which equates to £6,000. be very aware of arrangements fees!

Another potential pitfall when doing your sums is the void period. Empty properties yield no income and can damage your investment. Generally speaking, flats are better investments as they have lower void periods. The key is to ensure that you build up a balanced portfolio, buy a number of smaller units than one large one, in order to minimize void loss. When it comes to raising a mortgage, age is a factor. many lenders impose a maximum age cap of 70 or 75 at the end of the mortgage term although others are less strict. For example, one building society, Kent reliance, can lend to a maximum age of 85. Another factor which affects lenders decisions is where the property is located. Buy-to-let lenders won't be keen to lend on all types of property in any area, even if the sums stack up. Lenders will place restrictions on certain types of properties, such as flats above commercial premises, such as takeaways and so on. the main factor here is resaleability.

Stamp duty

What is stamp duty and who pays it?

Stamp Duty — Stamp Duty Land Tax (SDLT) official jargon — is a tax you pay when you buy a home. The buyer pays stamp duty – not the person selling. Stamp duty applies to both freehold and leasehold purchases over £125,000

2. How much do I have to pay?

Stamp duty used to be charged on the whole property price, so that it went up in big jumps. For example, if you bought a property for £250,000 you would have paid £2500 stamp duty; but if you bought a house costing just £1 more, you would tip into the next stamp duty bracket (what used to be 3%) and pay £7500 – a £5000 jump. This slab structure is gone now and from December 4, 2014 stamp duty is applied like income tax.

Stamp duty is charged according to the scale overleaf.

Purchase price of property	Stamp duty rate
Up to £125,000	Zero
Over £125,000 to £250,000	2%
Over £250,000 to £925,000	5%
Over £925,000 to £1.5 million	10%
Over £1.5 million	12%

So, for example, if the agreed purchase price is £275,000, under the new rules, stamp duty is calculated:

0% on the first £125,000 = £0
2% on the next £125,000 = £2,500
5% on the final £ 25,000 = £1,250
Total stamp duty payable = £3,750

Capital gains tax

Householders can currently sell their main residence and its grounds free from capital gains tax if the garden is less than half a hectare (1.23 acres). Even if the grounds are bigger, full relief can be obtained if the owner can show that they are " required for the reasonable enjoyment of the house as a residence". However, HMRC is making it harder to claim above the limit by cross checking all sales with stamp duty records. Essentially, in these straitened times, HMRC are looking to collect as much revenue as possible and property sales is one area on which they are concentrating.

Energy Performance Certificates (EPC's)

EPC's are compulsory for all rental homes (from 1st October 2008). Therefore all landlords are required to commission an EPC.

As seen above, an EPC surveyor will assess the property and looks at all the ways a house or flat can waste heat, such as inadequate loft insulation, lack of cavity wall insulation, draughts and obsolete boilers. After the assessment they will award a rating from A (as good as it gets) to G (terrible). The document also includes information and advice on how to improve matters, such as lagging the water tank or installing double-glazing. An EPC costs between £120-130 and is valid for ten years. Improvements made while the certificate is in force will not need a new survey.

Examples

There are three examples presented below which will enable the potential investor to get an idea of what problems might be inherent in a range of properties. Obviously, these are three isolated examples but you will get an idea of what to expect.

Example 1.

The city-centre Flat

Type of house: A two-bedroom flat, built in 1993.

Location: the Jewellery Quarter Birmingham.

Current energy efficient rating: 80% (C)

Potential energy efficiency rating:

82% (B)

Current bills: £198 per year

Potential savings per year: £13

Main failings: Manually controlled heating.

Proposed improvements typically costing less than £500. None

Proposed improvements typically costing more than £500. Install automatically controlled fan-assisted storage heaters, at a cost of about £1,000 for a property of this size (saving £13 per year)

The Georgian Farmhouse

Type of house: Five-bedroom farmhouse, built around 1800.

Location: Ratlinghope near Shrewsbury Shropshire.

Current energy efficiency rating: 30% (F)

Potential energy efficiency rating: 48% (E)

Potential savings: £550 per year.

Main failings: Solid stone walls are not good insulators, the main floor is built directly onto the earth, leaking heat. Only 20% of the windows are double glazed. There is only one energy efficient light bulb.

Proposed improvements costing less than £500. Add 2inches of insulation to the stone walls, at a cost of about £40m square (saving £470 per year) top up loft insulation to 250mm, costing about £240 (saving £58 per year) install low energy lighting (saving £15 per year).

Proposed improvements typically costing £500 or more. Change all windows to double glazing, costing about £350 per window (saving £39 per year) install photovoltaic cells-a typical domestic system costs between £10,000 and £18,000 to install, saving £68 per year.

The London terrace

Type of house: A four-bedroom terraced house built in 1912.

Location: Wandsworth, south London.
Current energy efficient rating: 56% (D).
Current bills: £952 per year.
Potential energy efficient rating: 56% (D).
Potential savings: £247 per year.

Main failings: Solid brick walls without insulation; suspended timber floor; no low-energy lighting; no individually controllable radiators; only 55% double glazing; non-condensing gas boiler.

Proposed improvements typically costing less than £500. Add 2inches of insulation to solid walls, at a cost of about £40 per m2 (saving £170 per year); top up loft insulation by 250mm-cost £240, saving £30 per year; add insulation to hot water tank and pipe-work costing about £300, saving about £19 per year.

Proposed improvements typically costing more than £500 per year. Install thermostatic radiator valves, which cost £250-£300 per radiator saving about £39 per year. Further improvements could be made installing solar water heating-a domestic system will cost £3000-£4,500 to install saving £17 per year.

The above examples were extracted from actual reports and will give an indication of cost and required improvements for specific property types.

Structural surveys

The basic structural survey is the homebuyers' survey and valuation, which is normally carried out by the building society or other lender and it will cost you between £200-350 and is not really an in-depth survey, merely allowing the lender to see whether they should lend or not and how much they should lend. Sometimes lenders keep what they refer to as a retention, which means that they will not forward the full value (less deposit) until certain defined works have been carried out.

If you want to go further than a homebuyers report, and the seller has not included a survey as part of the Home Information Pack (see below) then you will have to instruct a firm of surveyors who have several survey types, depending on how far you want to go and how much you want to spend.

A word of caution. Many people go rushing headlong into buying a flat or house. If you stop and think about this, it is complete folly and can prove very expensive later. A house or flat is a commodity like other commodities, except that it is usually a lot more expensive. A lot can be wrong with the commodity that you have purchased which is not immediately obvious. Only after you have completed the deal and paid over the odds for your purchase do you begin to regret what you have done.

The true market price of a property is not what the estate agent is asking, certainly not what the seller is asking. The true market price is the difference between what a property similar to the one in good condition is being sold at and your property minus cost of works to bring it up to that value.

Therefore, if you have any doubts whatsoever, and if you can afford it, get a detailed survey of the property you are proposing to buy and get the works that are required costed out. When negotiating, this survey is an essential tool in order to arrive at an accurate and fair price. Do not rest faith in others, particularly when you alone stand to lose.

One further word of caution. As stated, a lot of problems with property cannot be seen. A structural survey will highlight those. In some cases it may not be wise to proceed at all.

Legal costs

You should factor in conveyancing costs which can be anything from £500-£1500 depending on the property that you purchase. The solicitor that you employ will give you an idea of the disbursements over and above the basic cost. These disbursements will cover searches of local authorities and utility companies plus other searches as necessary.

Now read the main points from chapter two overleaf.

****

Main points from chapter two

- Give careful thought to all the costs of buying property.
- Banks dealing with buy to let mortgages will normally lend between 65-75% of the purchase price of a property. The more that you lend the more it costs. Banks have tightened their lending criteria considerably following the credit crunch.
- If the house or flat costs over £125,000, stamp duty will be payable. However, the old slab system has been replaced by a new system which is seen as more equitable.
- You should consider very carefully the need for a full structural survey when buying a property.
- Always bargain, never offer the asking price.

****

Chapter 3

Finding and Buying a Suitable Property

Having looked at the costs of acquiring a property, we need now to look at the type of property that you might want to invest in and also the areas that you should look in. Obviously, where you choose to buy your property will be your own decision. However, it may be your first time and you may be at a loss as to where to buy, i.e. rural areas or urban areas, the type and cost of property or whether a house or flat. There are several considerations here. The main consideration for a buy-to-let property is the letting potential and security of your asset, i.e. will it appreciate or will it depreciate. As mentioned in the previous chapter, flats are a better investment than houses, as a rule of thumb.

Area

Buying in a built up area has its advantages and disadvantages. There is usually more demand for property in a built up area. As far as letting is concerned, there are obvious advantages in that there are normally more close communities, because of the sheer density. Local services are closer to hand and there is a greater variety of housing for sale. Transport links are also usually quite good and there are normally plenty of shops.

Disadvantages are less space, less privacy, more local activity, noise and pollution, less street parking, more expensive insurance and different schooling environments to rural environments. The incidence of crime and vandalism and levels of overall stress are higher in built up, more urban areas. This is not the case with all built up areas. It is up to the buyer to carry out research before making a commitment.

If you are thinking of buying to let in a rural area, you might want to consider the following:

There is more detached housing with land, more space and privacy. There is also cleaner air and insurance premiums can be lower.

Disadvantages can be isolation, loneliness, lower level of services generally, limited choice of local education, therefore the property will be harder to let.

Choosing your property

You should think carefully when considering purchasing a larger property. You may encounter higher costs prior to letting, and also costs that may deter the would be tenant, which may include:

- Larger more expensive carpeting.
- More furniture. If you are letting your property furnished then you will need to outlay more at the outset.
- Larger gardens to tend. Although this may have been one of the attractions, large gardens are time consuming, expensive and hard work.
- Bigger bills.
- More decorating.
- Higher overall maintenance costs.

Purchasing a flat

There are some important points to remember when purchasing a flat. These are common points that are overlooked. For example, if you are buying a flat in a block that is leasehold you will need permission to sublet. This may pose difficulties depending on the freeholder.

Service charges. If you purchase a flat in a block, the costs of maintenance of the flat will be your own.

However, the costs of maintaining the common parts will be down to the landlord (usually) paid for by you through a service charge.

There has been an awful lot of trouble with service charges, trouble between landlord and leaseholder. It has to be said that many landlords see service charges as a way of making profit over and above other income, which is usually negligible after sale of a lease. Many landlords will own the companies that carry out the work and retain the profit made by these companies. They will charge leaseholders excessively for works, which are often not needed. The 1996 Housing Act, amended by the 2002 Commonhold and Leasehold Reform Act, attempts to strengthen the hand of leaseholders against unscrupulous landlords by making it very difficult indeed for landlords to take legal action for forfeiture (repossession) of lease without first giving the leaseholder a chance to challenge the service charges. In addition, the Acts place an obligation on landlords to be more transparent by producing more detailed accounts and information.

Be very careful if you are considering buying a flat in a block. You should establish levels of service charges and look at accounts. Try to elicit information from other leaseholders.

It could be that there is a leaseholders organisation, formed to manage their own service charges. This will give you direct control over contracts such as gardening, cleaning, maintenance contracts and cyclical decoration contracts. Better value for money is obtained in this way. In this case, at least you know that the levels will be fair, as no one leaseholder stands to profit. All of the above should be considered as the profit that you make from letting your property can be greatly diminished by extra costs such as maintenance charges to a freeholder.

Leasehold Reform Act 1993

Under this Act, as amended by The Commonhold and Leasehold Reform Act 2002, all leaseholders have the right to extend the length of their lease by a term of 90 years. For example, if your lease has 80 years left to run you can extend it to 170 Years. There is a procedure in the above Act for valuation. Leaseholders can collectively also purchase the freehold of the block.

There is a procedure for doing this in the Act although it is often time consuming and can be expensive. There are advantages however, particularly when leaseholders are not satisfied with management.

Viewing properties

Before you start house hunting, draw up a list of characteristics you will need from a property, such as the number of bedrooms, size of kitchen, garage and study and garden. Take the estate agents details with you when viewing. Also, take a tape measure with you.

Assess the location of the property. Look at all the aspects and the surroundings. Give some thought as to the impact this will have on the ability to rent. Assess the building. Check the facing aspect of the property, i.e., north, south etc. Check the exterior carefully. Look for a damp proof course - normally about 15cm from the ground. Look for damp inside and out. Items like leaking rainwater pipes should be noted, as they can be a cause of damp. Look carefully at the windows. Are they rotten? Do they need replacing and so on. Look for any cracks. These should most certainly be investigated. A crack can be symptomatic of something worse or it can merely be surface. If you are not in a position to make this judgment then others should make it for you.

Heating is important. If the house or flat has central heating you will need to know when it was last tested. Gas central heating should be tested at least once a year. All in all you need to remember that you cannot see everything in a house, particularly on the first visit. A great deal may be being concealed from you. In addition, your own knowledge of property may be slim. A second opinion is a must.

Buying a listed building

Buildings of architectural or historical interest are listed by the Secretary of State for National Heritage following consultation with English Heritage, to protect them against inappropriate alteration. In Wales, buildings are listed by the Secretary of State for Wales in consultation with CADW (Heritage Wales). In Scotland, they are listed by the Secretary of State for Scotland, in consultation with Historic Scotland. If you intend to carry out work to a listed building, you are likely to need listed building consent for any internal or external work, in addition to planning permission. The conservation officer in the local planning department can provide further information.

Buildings in conservation areas

Local authorities can designate areas of special architectural or historical significance. Conservation areas are protected to ensure that their character or interest is retained. Whole towns or villages may be conservation areas or simply one particular street.

Strict regulations are laid down for conservation areas. Protection includes all buildings and all types of trees that are larger than 7cm across at 1.5m above the ground. There may be limitations for putting up signs, outbuilding or items such as satellite dishes. Any developments in the area usually have to meet strict criteria, such as the use of traditional or local materials.

This also applies to property in national parks, designated areas of outstanding natural beauty and the Norfolk or Suffolk Broads.

Whether or not a property is listed or is deemed to be in a conservation area will show up when your conveyancer carries out the local authority search.

Buying a new house

There are a number of benefits to buying a new house. You have the advantages of being the first owner. There should not be a demand for too much maintenance or DIY jobs, as the building is new.

There will however be a defects period, which usually runs for 6 months for building and 12 months for electrical mechanical.

During this period you should expect minor problems, such as cracking of walls, plumbing etc, which will be the responsibility of the builder.

Energy loss will be minimal. A new house today uses 50 per cent less energy than a house built 15 years ago; consider the savings over an older property. An energy rating indicates how energy efficient a house is. The National House Building Council uses a rating scheme based on The National Energy Services Scheme, in which houses are given a rating between 0 and 10. A house rated 10 will be very energy efficient and have very low running costs for its size. In addition, an Energy Performance Certificate is mandatory, as described earlier. Security and safety are built in to new houses, smoke alarms are standard and security locks on doors and windows are usually included.

When the house market is slow, developers usually offer incentives to buyers, such as cash back, payment of deposit etc.

Building Guarantees

All new houses should be built to certain standards and qualify for one of the building industry guarantees. These building guarantees are normally essential for you to obtain a mortgage and they also make the property attractive to purchasers when you sell. A typical guarantee is the National House Building Council Guarantee (NHBCG).

The process of buying a property

Having considered the costs of the acquisition of a property, the next step is to find the property you want. For the investor, as well as all the considerations listed below, the return on investment will be a key priority.

Looking for a property is a long and sometimes dispiriting process. Trudging around estate agents, sorting through mountains of literature, dealing with estate agents details, scouring the papers and walking the streets. However, most of us find the property we want at the end of the day. It is then that we can put in our offer.

Making an offer

You should put your offer in to the estate agent or direct to the seller, depending on who you are buying from. As discussed earlier, your offer should be based on sound judgment, on what the property is worth and how much rental income after costs that you can derive from it, not on your desire to secure the property at any cost. A survey will help you to arrive at a schedule of works and cost. If you cannot afford to employ a surveyor from a high street firm then you should try to enlist other help. In addition, you should take a long and careful look at the house yourself, not just a cursory glance. Look at everything and try to get an idea of the likely cost to you of rectifying defects. However, I cannot stress enough the importance of getting a detailed survey.

Eventually, you will be in a position to make an offer for the property. You should base this offer on sound judgment. You should make it clear that your offer is subject to contract and survey (if you require further examination or wish to carry out a survey after the offer).

Exchange of contracts

Once the buyer and seller are happy with all the details stated in the contract and your conveyancer can confirm that there are no outstanding legal queries, there will be an exchange of contracts. The sale is now legally binding for both parties. You should arrange the necessary insurances, buildings and contents from this moment on, as you are now responsible for the property.

Completing a sale

This is the final day of the sale and normally takes place around ten days after exchange. Exchange and completion can take place on the same day if necessary but this is unusual. On the day of completion, you are entitled to vacant possession and you will receive the keys.

Now read the main points from chapter 3 overleaf.

Main points from chapter three

- When looking for a house, consider essential points such as area and services and the impact these will have on letting.

- Think carefully about costs involved and also work if you are considering buying a larger property.

- When purchasing a flat, consider maintenance charges as these can eat into your profit.

- Before viewing, draw up a list of characteristics you will need from a house or flat.

- There are a number of advantages to buying a new house, such as new construction and minimal energy loss.

****

Chapter 4

Buying a Property at an Auction

Although many people will go through the traditional route of acquiring buy-to-let property through an estate agent, there are other routes, one main one being the auction. Buying at auction requires a different set of skills and you need to know what you are buying, where it is and what the problems are, if any. Why is it being sold at auction? Certainly, you need to act fairly quickly as you need to inspect the property before auction day, arrive at the final bid price that you will not exceed and be prepared to complete within 28 days.

What is a property auction?

The process is very similar to the normal method of private sale. However, for an auction sale the seller and their solicitor carry out all the necessary paperwork and legal investigations prior to the auction. Subject to the property receiving an acceptable bid, the property will be 'sold' on auction day with a legally binding exchange of contracts and a fixed completion date.

Different types of property auction houses

Auction houses vary in size and the amount of business that they conduct and the frequency with which they hold auctions. Most will sell both residential and commercial property and each will have its own style of operation, and fee structure. Large auction houses will hold auctions frequently, perhaps every two months and will have around 250 lots for sale. A lot of the auctions happen in London. Most of the large auction houses will deal with property put forward by large institutions, such as banks selling repossessions.

Also local authorities and will advertise the sales in the mainstream media and trade papers. The medium size auction houses will hold auctions as frequently as they can, in regional venues, such as racecourses and conference centres, and depending on stock, usually every two to three months, tending to advertise locally. The small auction houses will have far fewer lots and will hold their sales in smaller local venues. They may advertise in local press but more often will trade on word of mouth.

Those who attend auctions

As you might imagine, all sorts of people attend auctions. The common denominator is that they are all interested in buying property.

Property investors are most common at auction, people who are starting out building a portfolio or those who have large portfolios that they wish to expand. They tend to fall into two groups, those who are after capital appreciation, i.e. buy at a low value and build the capital value and those who are looking for rental income. Then there are the property traders who like a quick profit from buying and 'flipping' property. These types usually have intimate knowledge of an area and are well placed to make a quick profit. Then we have the developers who look for small profitable sites or larger sites where property can be built and sold on. The sites can have existing buildings on them or can be vacant lots with or without planning permission. Last, but not least, we have those people who intend to buy solely for the purpose of owner occupation, look to buy a below- value property that they can redesign and make their own.

What types of property are suitable for auction?

There is strong demand for all types of properties offered at auction. These may be properties requiring updating, those with short leases, development sites with or without planning permission, repossessions, forced sales and, investment properties. Also ground rents, probates, receivership sales and local authority properties.

However, any type of property can be sold at auction and initially the property will be inspected to discuss specific criteria and the current situation. Extensive research will be carried out by the auction house and advice offered as to whether auction is the appropriate method of sale. The below represents a cross section of what might be found at auction.

Properties for Improvement

Properties in need of updating make ideal auction Lots. They are in great demand from refurbishment specialists and private buyers, keen to undertake a project for their own occupation or for resale. They also appeal to buy-to-let investors who carry out the improvements then retain them as part of a property portfolio.

Tenanted Properties

Residential houses and flats with tenants in residence sell well at auction. Notice doesn't need to be served on tenants, and rental income continues to be received right up to completion.

Residential Investments

Houses in multiple occupation and blocks of flats are sold at auction as valuable investments. Here it is the rent level that determines the sale price, just as much as the building itself.

Development Propositions

Derelict or disused farm buildings, empty commercial premises, buildings with potential for conversion or change of use, can all sell well at auction. In some locations a change to residential can significantly add to the value of a property, in other situations there may be space for additional dwellings or to substantially enlarge the property.

Building Land

There is no better way of ensuring a seller achieves best price for a building plot or parcel of development land than to offer it for sale by auction. Builders will be able to consult with architects, planners etc., and be ready to bid in the auction room.

Mixed-Use Properties

Properties that have twin uses or a variety of potential future uses are ideal for sale by auction. Retail shops with accommodation above appeal to investors as well as owner-occupiers. Further conversion work can often be undertaken and the property tailored to suit the purchaser's special requirements.

Commercial Investments

Retail shops, offices, industrial units, garage blocks and parking areas - an ever increasing number of commercial investments are being sold at auction. It doesn't matter whether they are vacant or tenanted, with lease renewal soon needed or with a long way to run.

Unique Properties

There are always some rare entries, sought after property and prime locations that need to be sold in a competitive bidding environment. Unexpectedly high prices have been achieved by this route.

Amenity Land and Other Property

Paddocks, meadows, fields, moorings, amenity land and also other unusual land parcels are all sold at auction. If it is property or land that is surplus to requirements, the likelihood is a buyer can be found at auction.

Why is property being sold at an auction?

There are a number of reasons why property is sold at an auction:

- A quick sale is needed, often due to the owner being in financial difficulties or it is a repossession
- There are structural problems which prevent the property being sold easily in the conventional manner.
- Properties sold by public bodies. Here you get all sort of property, including weird and wonderful properties such as public toilets and police stations, all of which may have their uses.
- The property is unique and there are no direct comparisons, such as lighthouses and the above mentioned public toilet.

It is always best to find out why exactly the property is being sold at auction. Is it so difficult to get rid of because of some inherent reason? Ask why is this property at auction and not being sold in the conventional way? Who exactly is the vendor and what if any are the problems stopping it being sold conventionally? The reasons that the property is at auction may be entirely innocent but it is always worth finding out to avoid future problems.

What happens next?

Once you have found your auction, to receive a complimentary auction catalogue you should contact the Auctioneers and this will give the information about the properties being offered for sale. You can also download a catalogue from the auctioneers website. The catalogue includes descriptions of the available properties, legal information, viewing arrangements and a guide price, which is purely an indication of a realistic selling price. This should not be taken as a firm asking or selling price and should be relied upon as a guide only. Professional advice must be taken in relation to any lot in which there is an interest.

For lots where viewings are arranged, these are carried out on a block basis and are published in all advertising and in the auction catalogue.

Any prospective purchaser is welcome at these viewings and should the scheduled appointments be inconvenient, alternative arrangements can be made. Any interest must be registered with the Auctioneers in order that prospective purchasers may be kept informed as to the progress of the sale.

Bidding for a property

The lots will be offered and the bidding taken to the highest possible level and once the gavel falls, the contracts will be exchanged. The buyer purchases the property at the price they bid - this cannot be negotiated and the stipulated terms cannot be changed. The buyer will then pay 10% of the purchase price on the day and completion occur 28 days later. The funds are then paid to the seller less the fees of the Auctioneers and those of the seller's solicitor.

The atmosphere of an auction room can be extremely exciting and competitive and it is often the case that an interested party will bid in excess of the figure that had previously been set as their maximum. In some cases, the prices achieved at auction can be higher than those achieved by private treaty.

The seller will provide a legal pack that may be inspected at any time. Auctioneers will strongly advise that professional advice is obtained from a legal representative. Details of the seller's solicitors will be available and, should a mortgage be required, it is advisable to have this in place prior to the sale. Again, Auctioneers strongly advise that funding is discussed with a professional advisor prior to attending the sale.

The successful buyer will be required to pay 10% of the purchase price on the day, together with a buyer's premium which is normally £250 including VAT.

The balance of the purchase price is required on the agreed completion day and this is normally 28 days after the auction, however this can vary so best to check with the auction house.

How do prospective purchasers find out legal and survey information for the properties in which they are interested?

A legal pack is requested from each of the vendor's solicitors and this contains copies of all legal papers, which will be required by any prospective purchasers for them to make an informed decision regarding the purchase of any lot.

The pack will include office copy entries and plans, the relevant local authority search, leases (if applicable), Special Conditions of Sale, replies to pre-contract enquiries and any other relevant documents. A copy of these legal packs can usually be obtained from auctioneers for a small charge. Should any additional information be required, the seller's solicitors are listed in the catalogue and can be contacted directly. All legal packs are available for inspection at each auction.

Any purchase at auction takes place under the assumption that documentation and the terms of the contract have been read.

It is strongly recommended that any potential purchasers carry out full investigations for any lot in which they have an interest and a survey is an integral part of that investigation.

How is finance arranged?

Should a mortgage be required, approval in principle must be obtained prior to auction. Lenders are now familiar with the auction process and are usually willing to provide a mortgage offer for buyers intending to purchase at auction. A valuation and survey will be required along with legal evidence that there are no issues that will affect the value.

It is essential that the lender can provide funds within the timescale for completion. On the day of the auction, the purchaser will need to pay 10% of the purchase price and must ensure there are cleared funds to pay this amount. Sometimes, finance can be arranged through an Auctioneers on request.

Can lots be bought before auction?

Vendors may consider offers submitted before auction day. Any such offers need to be submitted in writing to an Auctioneers - this will be referred to the vendor and their instruction will be passed on to the prospective purchaser. Any offers will have to be unconditional and the buyer must be in a position to exchange contracts and pay the required deposit before auction day. With most auctioneers, no offers are considered within five days of the auction.

What should I take with me to the auction room?

The items required are as follows:

- Deposit cheque or banker's draft for any potential purchase
- Identification - this is legally required under the money laundering regulations. Therefore a driving licence or passport is required and a current utility bill to show proof of residence.
- Details of solicitors acting on behalf of any potential purchaser.

What happens if a prospective purchaser is unable to attend the auction?

If prospective purchasers are unable to attend the sale, it is possible to bid in other ways:

- By telephone - the interested party will be telephoned as the lot is being auctioned.
- By proxy in writing - a member of the auction team will represent the buyer, who has previously specified their maximum bid

In each case a registration form and cheque to cover the deposit and buyer's fee, are required prior to the date of the auction. A bidder's registration form is printed in the catalogue or alternatively can be obtained from the office

Will the property be insured when I purchase?

No - the purchaser at auction is responsible for obtaining Building insurance cover from the moment the property is deemed sold to them at auction.

Now read the main points from chapter four overleaf.

****

Main points from chapter 4

- Buying at auction is an assured way of securing a purchase. Once a bid is accepted, contracts will be exchanged on the day of the sale. The seller cannot withdraw from the sale, nor is it possible for any kind of gazumping to take place.
- Due to auctions being conducted in public, there can be no secret bidding or unfair competition and once the gavel comes down, the successful bidder is legally committed to both pay the agreed price and complete the purchase.
- It is always best to find out why exactly the property is being sold at auction. Is it so difficult to get rid of because of some inherent reason. Ask why is this property at auction and not being sold in the conventional way? Who exactly is the vendor and what if any are the problems stopping it being sold conventionally?
- Once you have found your auction, to receive a complimentary auction catalogue you should contact the Auctioneers and this will give the information about the properties being offered for sale. You can also download a catalogue from the auctioneers website.
- Buyers should check the day before the auction that any required lots are still available. Early arrival at the auction is recommended to ensure the Auctioneer's announcement are noted regarding withdrawn lots and changes in the order of the sale.

****

Chapter 5

Finding Tenants and Managing Your Property

A lot of time, effort and money has gone into finding a property and getting it ready to let. Now you want a return on your investment. The return will come from an increase in capital value and, most importantly, from a tenant. It is therefore vital that you find the right tenant and that rental payments are guaranteed.

So, having laid out your business plan, based on the considerations outlined in chapter one, and given much thought to the purchase of a property to let, it is now necessary to look at the possible sources of the tenant for your property and also the ongoing management. Remember, the tenant is the key to your future income and profit and also to your own personal peace or otherwise and therefore must be chosen extremely carefully.

On the basis of your business plan you will know the type of person that you are prepared to accept because you will have identified what type of management scenario you wish. You will know their position, i.e., whether professional, student, working or on benefits or retired. In order to locate this person you will need to know the various sources available to you. In addition to sourcing the ideal tenant, you will want to know that your rent is being collected and the property managed properly. This can be a headache if you choose the wrong agent.

Letting Agents

An amendment to the Enterprise and Regulatory Reform Act 2013 enabled the Government to require agents to sign up to a redress scheme.

The Redress Scheme for Lettings Agency Work and Property Management Work (Requirement to Belong to a Scheme etc) (England) Order 2014 made membership of a scheme a legal requirement with effect from 1 October 2014. The Government also amended the Consumer Rights Act 2015 to require letting agents to publish a full tariff of their fees. If you intend to use an agent to manage your properties then ensure that it is signed up to a redress scheme. One such scheme is The Property Ombudsman Scheme, described below. This is an extract from their Code.

Why should you choose an agent who is registered with TPO?

- Registered agents must follow The Property Ombudsman Letting Code of Practice. This sets out the framework within which registered agents must operate and the standards of service they must provide for both tenants and landlords.
- The Code is compulsory and is rigorously applied in our complaints handling.
- The agent is required and has agreed to have Professional Indemnity insurance to ensure that any compensation awarded to you can be paid.
- The agent is required and has agreed to have an in-house complaints system with written procedures; inform you how to refer any unresolved dispute to the Ombudsman and co-operate with any investigation by the Ombudsman.
- The agent agrees to pay compensation, in full and final settlement of a complaint, if this is awarded by the Ombudsman and is accepted by you as the complainant. This award must be paid promptly. The maximum that the Ombudsman can award is £25,000. In the rare case that an agent fails repeatedly to follow the rules of the scheme, the agent can be reprimanded, fined or expelled. The TPO Code of Practice requires agents to meet all their legal obligations.

- This includes: Duty of care. An agent must always work in the best interests of the client, that is to say the person who is paying for the letting agency services (usually the landlord). But the agent must also always treat fairly, and with courtesy, all those involved in the proposed renting or letting. If the agent or one of its staff has any personal or business interest in the property, the landlord must be told.
- Impartiality. An agent must make sure that no tenants or landlords are disadvantaged because they are unfamiliar with any aspect of the letting process. An agent will offer appropriate explanations and assistance to all, regardless of age, race, religious belief, gender, sexuality, ethnicity or disability.
- Access. An agent must keep accurate records of keys held, and inform current tenants of any access required, except in cases of genuine emergency.

What else can tenants expect from a TPO registered letting agent?

- **Offers**. When an offer has been accepted but before the tenancy agreement is in force the agent must inform the applicant whether or not marketing is to continue.
- **Deposits**. Any deposit that the tenant may be required to pay at the beginning of a tenancy which is held by the agent must be held in a client account.
- Where the law requires it, any deposit taken on an Assured Shorthold Tenancy should be transferred within 30 days to an approved TDS.
- **Tenancy Agreement**. Tenants should expect to be supplied with a draft Tenancy Agreement to read before signing, recording the terms of the letting.
- **Inventory**. The agent should ensure that the tenant receives an inventory of furniture, fittings and equipment at the beginning of the tenancy.

- This will record the condition of the property and/or contents.

What else can landlords expect from a TPO registered agent?

- **Recommended Rents**. The rental figure given by the agent must represent current market conditions. The agent must be able to support any figure given, and, wherever possible, it must be based on comparisons with similar properties in a similar location.
- **Terms of Business**. The agent must provide written Terms of Business that confirm the landlord's requirements and clearly state and explain all fees and charges.
- **Marketing your Property**. The agent must comply with various requirements about how 'To Let' boards are displayed, how viewings are conducted, and whether marketing should continue after an offer is received.
- **Viewings**. The agent must follow the landlord's instructions on how viewings should be conducted. He will record and pass on to the landlord any feedback from viewings.
- **References**. The agent will take due care in obtaining the references of potential tenants.

How do you tell if a letting agent is a TPO registered letting agent?

All agents must display the TPO logo on windows, advertising and stationery. If you need help in finding an agent you can contact the Ombudsman's office or look at the TPO website www.tpos.co.uk.
All agents are required to display copies of the TPO Consumer Guide in their office and make copies available, free of charge, on request.

If you do decide to use an agent, there are obvious advantages: they are likely to have tenants on their books: they are likely to be experienced and can vet tenants properly before signing a tenancy; they can provide you with a tenancy agreement.

They can also provide a service after the property is let. However, agents charge for this service and their fees can vary enormously. It is up to you as a would-be landlord to ensure you understand what it is they are charging and exactly what you are left with after the charges. Some agencies will offer a guaranteed income for the duration of the contract that you have signed with them, even if a tenant leaves. However, you should be extremely careful as a number of cases recently against such agencies have revealed that there are unscrupulous operators around.

Online lettings agents

The rise of online lettings agents has been rapid and they now account for 3.5% of the market. The attractions are obvious, the costs. One of the biggest online property agents, EasyProperty.com offers 'pick and mix' services ranging from £10 a week for adverts on Right Move, Prime Location and Zoopla to 3% commission for full property management. For tenant finding with all the frills, such as hosted viewings and professional photos to check-in the total bill would be £445. This equates to less than half the commission charged by high-street agents. Another agent, Purplebricks.com is also very competitive. However, there can be drawbacks.

The main drawback is accessibility. If you have your contract with a local agent, they will be there when you want them. Online tends to be one step removed. You are strongly advised to consider what it is you want before entering into any deal with an online agent. If you do appoint an agent to manage a property you should agree at the outset, in writing, exactly what constitutes management.

Failure to understand the deal can cost you dearly. For example, in a lot of cases, an agent will charge you a fixed fee, sometimes 1 months rental, for finding a tenant, but will then exercise the right that they have given themselves in the initial contract to sign a new agreement and charge another months rent after the tenancy has expired.

In this way they will charge you a months rent every six months for doing nothing at all.

Agents will typically look after the following:

1 Transfer the utility bills and the council tax into the name of the tenant. Sign agreements and take up references.
2 Paying for repairs, although an agent will only normally do this if rent is being paid directly to them and they can make appropriate deductions.
3 Chase rent arrears.
4 Serve notices of intent to seek possession if the landlord instructs them to do so. An agent cannot commence court proceedings except through a solicitor.
5 Visit the property at regular intervals and check that the tenants are not causing any damage.
6 Dealing with neighbour complaints.
7 Banking rental receipts if the landlord is abroad
8 Dealing with housing benefit departments if necessary. The extent to which agents actually do any or all of the above really depends on the caliber of the agent. It also depends on the type of agreement you have with the agent. Like your initial business plan, you should be very clear about what it is you want from the agent and how much they charge.

Beware! There are many so-called rental agencies, which have sprang up since the property recession and also the advent of "Buy to Let". These agents are not professional, do not know a thing about property management, are shady and should be avoided like the plague. Shop around and seek a reputable agent. A typical management fee might be 10-15 percent of the rent, although there is lots of competition and lower prices can be obtained.

As stated, there are many ways of charging and you should be clear about this. It is illegal for agencies to charge tenants for giving out a landlord's name/address. Most agencies will charge the landlord.

Advertisements

If you decide to dispense with the use of an agent, the classified advertisement section of local papers is a good place to seek potential tenants. Local papers are obviously cheaper than the nationals such as the Evening Standard in London or the broadsheets such as the Guardian. The type of newspaper you advertise in will largely reflect what type of customer you are looking for. An advert in the pages of the Times would indicate that you are looking for a well-heeled professional and this would be reflected in the type of property that you have to let. There are many free ad papers and also you may want to go to student halls of residence or hospitals in order to attract a potential tenant. When you do advertise, you should indicate clearly the type of property, in what area, what is required, i.e., male or female only, and the rent. You should try and avoid abbreviations as this causes confusion.

One consideration if looking for a tenant yourself, in October 2014, the new Immigration Act came into force which puts the responsibility on landlords to vet their tenants, or prospective tenants to check to see if they have a right to be in the country. More information can be obtained from www.gov.uk.

The public sector

One other source of income is the local authority or housing association. Quite often, your property will be taken off your hands under a five-year contract and you will receive a rental income paid direct for this period, with agreed increases. However, the local authority or housing association will demand a high standard before taking the property off your hands. Quite often the rent achieved will be lower than a comparable market rent, in return for full management.

In a secure income can be expected. If you wish to try this avenue then you should contact your local authority or nearest large association.

Company lets

Where the tenant is a company rather than an individual, the tenancy agreement will be similar to an assured shorthold but will not be bound by the six-month rule (see chapter eight for details of assured shorthold tenancies). Company lets can be from any length of time, from a week to several years, or as long as you like.

The major difference between contracts and standard assured shorthold agreements is that the contract will be tailored to individual needs, and the agreement is bound by the provisions of contract law. Company tenancies are bound by the provisions of contract law and not by the Housing Acts. Note: if you are considering letting to a company you must use a letting agent or solicitor. Most companies will insist on it. The advantages of a landlord letting to a company are:

- A company or embassy has no security of tenure and therefore cannot be a sitting tenant.
- A company cannot seek to reduce the rent by statutory interventions.
- Rental payments are often made quarterly or six monthly in advance.
- The financial status of a company is usually more secure than that of an individual.
- Company tenants often require long-term lets to accommodate staff relocating on contracts of between one and five years.

The main disadvantages of company lets are:

- A company tenancy can only be to a bona fide company or embassy. A tenancy to a partnership would not count as a company let and may have some security of tenure.

- If the tenant is a foreign government, the diplomatic status of the occupant must be ascertained, as the courts cannot enforce breaches of contract with somebody who possesses diplomatic immunity.
- A tenancy to a foreign company not registered in the UK may prove time consuming and costly if it becomes necessary to pursue claims for unpaid rent or damage through foreign courts.

Short-lets

Although company lets can be of any length, it is becoming increasingly popular for companies to rent flats from private landlords on short-lets. A short-let is any let of less than six months. But here, it is essential to check the rules with any borough concerned. Some boroughs will not allow lets for less than three months, as they do not want to encourage transient people in the neighborhood.

Generally speaking, short-lets are only applicable in large cities where there is a substantial shifting population. Business executives on temporary relocation, actors and others involved in television production or film work, contract workers and visiting academics are examples of people who might require a short-let.

From a landlord's point of view, short-lets are an excellent idea if you have to vacate your own home for seven or eight months, say, and do not want to leave it empty.

Short-let tenants provide useful extra income as well as keeping an eye on the place. Or if you are buying a new property and have not yet sold the old one, it can make good business sense to let it to a short-let tenant.

Short-let tenants are, usually, from a landlord's point of view, excellent blue-chip occupants. They are busy professionals, high earners, out all day and used to high standards. As the rent is paid by the company there is no worry for the landlord on this score either. A major plus of short-lets is that they command between 20-50 percent more rent than the optimum market rent for that type of property.

The one downside of short-lets is that no agency can guarantee permanent occupancy.

Student lets

Many mainstream letting agencies will not consider students and a lot of landlords similarly are not keen. There is the perception that students will not look after a home and tend to live a lifestyle guaranteed to increase the wear and tear on a property. However, if handled correctly, student lets can be profitable and a number of specialist companies have grown up which concentrate solely on students. Although students quite often want property for only eight or nine months, agencies that deal with students make them sign for a whole year. Rent is guaranteed by confirmation that the student is a genuine student with references from parents, who act as guarantors.

There can be a lot of money made from student lets. However, the tenancy will require more avid policing because of the nature of student lifestyle.

The DSS and housing benefit

Very few letting agencies or landlords will touch DSS or housing benefit tenants. However, as with student lets, there is another side of the coin. Quite often it is essential for a tenant on HB to have a guarantor, usually a homeowner, before signing a tenancy. Then it is up to the machinations of the benefit system to ensure that the landlord receives rent. The rent is assessed by a benefit officer, with the rent usually estimated at market price. There are rent levels set for each are that the benefit officer will not go above. At the time of writing the benefit system is undergoing significant changes which will have an adverse impact on those on housing benefit. This could also impact on those landlords who take tenants on HB. If you are going to take a tenant on HB then you will need to ensure that you are fully acquainted with the rules, in particular the bedroom tax, so that you can be sure of getting your rent.

A deposit is paid normally and rent is paid direct to the landlord. This will require the tenant's consent No other conditions should be accepted by a private landlord. Rent certainly should not be paid direct to the tenant.

Although tenants on HB have a bad name, due to stereotyping, there are many reasons why a person may be on benefit and if housing benefit tenancies are managed well, then this can be a useful source of tenant.

Holiday lets

Before the Housing Act 1988 became law, many landlords advertised their properties as holiday lets to bypass the then rules regarding security of tenure. Strictly speaking, a holiday let is a property let for no more than a month to any one tenant. If the same tenant renews for another month then the landlord is breaking the law. Nowadays, holiday lets must be just that; let for a genuine holiday. If you have a flat or cottage that you wish to let for holiday purposes, whether or not you live in it yourself for part of the year, you are entering into a quite different agreement with the tenant. Holiday lets are not covered by the Housing Act. The contract is finalised by exchange of letters with the tenant where they place a deposit and the owner confirms the booking. If the let is not for a genuine holiday you may have problems in evicting the tenant.

Generally speaking, certain services must be provided for the let to be deemed a holiday let. Cleaning services and changes of bed linen are essential. The amount paid by the holiday-maker will usually include utilities but would exclude use of the telephone, fax machine etc.

If you have a property that you think is suitable for holiday let or wish to invest in one, there are numerous companies who will put you on to their books.

However, standards are high and there are a certain number of criteria to be met, such as safety checks, before they will consider taking you on.

If possible, you should talk to someone with some experience of this type of let before entering into an agreement with an agency. The usual problems may arise, such as ensuring occupancy all year round and the maintenance of your property, which will be higher due to a high turnover. In addition to the above, the tax situation is changing for those with holiday lets which will mean the loss of certain allowances and the tightening up of others.

Bedsits

Bedsitting rooms are usually difficult to let and can cause problems. It is best to leave this area of letting alone unless you are experienced and well versed in this particular area. There are numerous regulations to adhere to. Houses in Multiple Occupation regulations are quite strict.

The Housing Act 2004 has introduced new tougher regulations for HMOs. If a landlord is letting out property in a block with more than three unrelated dwellings then a licence will be needed from the local authority before lettings can take place. You should contact your local authority if you are in this position. There is also a problem of high turnover. Leave this kind of letting to others and concentrate on houses or flats.

Showing the property to the tenant

Once you have found a tenant, the next stage is to make arrangements for viewing the property. It is a good idea to make all appointments on the same day in order to avoid wasting time. If you decide on a likely tenant, it is wise to take up references yourself if you are not using an agency who will do this for you. This will normally be a previous landlord's reference and also a bank reference plus a personal reference.

Only when these have been received and you have established that the person(s) is/are safe should you go ahead.

Make sure that no keys have been handed over until the cheque has been cleared and you are in receipt of a month's rent and a month's deposit.

Deposits-Tenancy Deposit Protection Scheme

The Tenancy Deposit Protection Scheme was introduced to protect all deposits paid to landlords after 6th April 2007. After this date, landlords and/or agents must use a government authorised scheme to protect deposits. The need for such a scheme has arisen because of the historical problem with deposits. The scheme works as follows:

Moving into a property

At the beginning of a new tenancy agreement, the tenant will pay a deposit to the landlord or agent as usual. Within 14 days the landlord is required to give the tenant details of how the deposit is going to be protected including:

- the contact details of the tenancy deposit scheme
- the contact details of landlord or agent
- how to apply for the release of the deposit
- what to do if there is a dispute about the deposit

There are three tenancy deposit schemes that a landlord can opt for:
Tenancy Deposit Solutions Ltd
www.mydeposits.co.uk
info@mydeposits.co.uk
The Tenancy Deposit Scheme
www.tds.gb.com
0845 226 7837
The Deposit Protection Service
www.depositprotection.com
0870 707 1 707

The schemes above fall into two categories, insurance based schemes and custodial schemes.

Custodial Scheme

- The tenant pays the deposit to the landlord
- The landlord pays the deposit into the scheme
- Within 14 days of receiving the deposit, the landlord must give the tenant prescribed information
- A the end of the tenancy, if the landlord and tenant have agreed how much of the deposit is to be returned, they will tell the scheme which returns the deposit, divided in the way agreed by the parties.
- If there is a dispute, the scheme will hold the disputed amount until the dispute resolution service or courts decide what is fair
- The interest accrued by deposits in the scheme will be used to pay for the running of the scheme and any surplus will be used to offer interest to the tenant, or landlord if the tenant isn't entitled to it.

Insurance based schemes

- The tenant pays the deposit to the landlord
- The landlord retains the deposit and pays a premium to the insurer (this is the key difference between the two schemes)
- Within 14 days of receiving a deposit the landlord must give the tenant prescribed information.
- At the end of the tenancy if the landlord and tenant agree how the deposit is to be divided or otherwise then the landlord will return the amount agreed

- If there is a dispute, the landlord must hand over the disputed amount to the scheme.

- If for any reason the landlord fails to comply, the insurance arrangements will ensure the return of the deposit to the tenant if they are entitled to it.

If a landlord or agent hasn't protected a deposit with one of the above then the tenant can apply to the local county court for an order for the landlord either to protect the deposit or repay it.

The Deregulation Act 2015

Since 6 April 2007, it has been mandatory for a landlord to ensure that a tenant's deposit that has been paid in respect of an assured shorthold tenancy (AST) is protected within a Tenancy Deposit Scheme. The Deregulation Act now extends the requirement to protect a deposit to AST's created before 6 April 2007 in certain circumstances. Landlords are now required to protect their deposits within a scheme before 23 June 2015 and serve the prescribed information relating to the deposit on the tenant. If a landlord fails to do this then it is prevented from recovering possession of the property from the tenant and is potentially liable for financial penalties.

Rental guarantees

The landlord is always advised to obtain a guarantor if there is any potential uncertainty as to payment of rent. One example is where the tenant is on benefits. The guarantor will be expected to assume responsibility for the rent if the tenant ceases to pay at any time during the term of the tenancy. There is a sample guarantee form in the appendix to this book.

Now read the main points from chapter five overleaf.

Main points from chapter five

- The right choice of tenant is crucial as this is the key to the return on your investment.

- You should make sure that you have all the facts about a letting agents terms and conditions before you enter into an agreement. make sure that the agent is a member of a recognised redress scheme, which is a legal requirement.

- The classified advertisement section in the local paper is a good place to seek potential tenants, especially if you wish to manage the property yourself.

- The public sector offers a full management service but often offer a lower rent.

- There are other avenues to explore, such as company lets, short lets, holiday lets and so on. Make sure that you fully understand the various markets and what each entails before entering into an agreement.

- Make sure that, when you have found a tenant that you take up references and a deposit, and ensure that the tenant is fully aware of all relevant details.

****

Chapter 6

What Should be Provided Under the Tenancy?

When you let a property, you have the choice of letting it furnished or unfurnished. There is a market for both but most properties will at least have white goods installed.

Furniture

A landlords decision whether or not to furnish property will depend on the sort of tenant that he is aiming to find. The actual legal distinction between a furnished property and an unfurnished property has faded into insignificance. If a landlord does let a property as furnished then the following would be the absolute minimum:

- Seating, such as a sofa and an armchair.
- Cabinet or sideboard.
- Kitchen tables and chairs.
- Cooker and refrigerator.
- Bedroom furniture.

Even unfurnished lets, however, are expected to come complete with a basic standard of furniture, particularly carpets and kitchen goods. If the landlord does supply electrical equipment then he or she will be responsible for carrying out annual checks along with annual checks on the boiler.

Services

Service charges, and the paying of these charges, will be the responsibility of the leaseholder.

They will be included in the rent charged by the leaseholder to the tenant of the flat. However, the leaseholder should have some idea of the law in this area as it will be a cost which needs to be considered.

Usually, a landlord (freeholder) will only provide services to a tenant if the property is a flat situated in a block or house split into flats or is a house on a private estate. The services will include cyclical painting and maintenance, usually on a three to four year basis (flats) and gardening and cleaning plus repairs to the communal areas, plus communal electricity bills and water rates. These services should be outlined in the agreement and administered within a strict framework of law. The 1985 Landlord and Tenant Act Section 18-30 as amended by the 1987 LTA and the 1996 Housing Act as amended by the 2002 Commonhold and Leasehold Reform Act are the main areas of law.

The landlord has rigid duties imposed within the Acts, such as the need to gain estimates before commencing works and also to consult with residents where the cost exceeds £250 per flat. The landlord must give the tenant 28 days notice of works to be carried out and a further 28 days to consider estimates, inviting feedback.

Tenants (leaseholders) have the right to see audited accounts and invoices relating to work. Service charges, as an extra payment over and above the rent are always contentious and it is an area that landlords need to be aware of if they are to manage professionally.

Insurance

Strictly speaking, there is no legal duty on either landlord or tenant to insure the property. However, it is highly advisable for the landlord to provide buildings insurance as he/she stands to lose a lot more in the event of fire or other disaster

In addition, mortgagors will always want insurance in place to protect their own investment. A landlord letting property for a first time would be well advised to consult his/her insurance company before letting as there are different criteria to observe when a property is let and not to inform the company could invalidate the policy.

At the end of the tenancy

The tenancy agreement will normally spell out the obligations of the tenant at the end of the term. Essentially, the tenant will have an obligation to:

- Have kept the interior clean and tidy and in a good state of repair and decoration.
- Have not caused any damage.
- Have replaced anything that they have broken.
- Replace or pay for the repair of anything that they have damaged.
- Pay for the laundering of the linen.
- Pay for any other laundering.
- Put anything that they have moved or removed back to how it was.

Sometimes a tenancy agreement will include for the tenants paying for anything that is soiled at their own expense, although sensible wear and tear is allowed for. The landlord will normally be able to recover any loss from the deposit that the tenant has given on entering the premises (see previous chapter for details of the Deposit Protection Schemes). However, sometimes, the tenants will withhold rent for the last month in order to recoup their deposit. The introduction of the Deposit Protection Schemes have made this more difficult in practice. It is up to the landlord to negotiate reimbursement for any damage caused, but this should be within reason. There is a remedy, which can be pursued in the small claims court if the tenants refuse to pay but this is rarely successful.

Now read the main points from chapter six.

Main points from chapter Six

- A landlord's decision to furnish a property will depend on the sort of tenant he is aiming to find.

- Even unfurnished lets are expected to come complete with a basic standard of furniture.

- Usually, the landlord (freeholder) will only supply services to a tenant if the flat is in a block or a house on a private estate.

- If services are provided tenants (leaseholders) have a right to audited accounts annually. The extra burden of service charges should be taken into account when letting the property.

****

Chapter 7

Knowing the Law

Explaining the law

Having traveled this far in finding a property and signed up the tenant, it is now time to understand a little more about the law. Purchasing a property is one thing but the ongoing management is a different ball game altogether and requires a wide knowledge base.

As a landlord or potential landlord it is very important to understand the rights and obligations of both yourself and your tenant, exactly what can and what cannot be done once the tenancy agreement has been signed and the tenant has moved into the property.

Some landlords think they can do exactly as they please, because the property belongs to them. Tenants often do not know any differently and therefore the landlord can, and often does, get away with breaking the law. However, if you are about to embark upon a career as a landlord then it is important that you have a grasp of the key principles of the law. In order to fully understand the law we should begin by looking at the main types of relationship between people and their homes.

The freehold and the lease

In law, there are two main types of ownership and occupation of property. These are: freehold and leasehold. These arrangements are very old indeed.

Freehold

If a person owns their property outright (usually with a mortgage) then they will be a freeholder. The only claims to ownership over and above their own might be those of the building society or the bank, which lent them the money to buy the place.

They will re-possess the property if the mortgage payments are not kept up with. In certain situations though, the local authority (council) for an area can affect a person's right to do what they please with their home even if they are a freeholder. This will occur when planning powers are exercised, for example, in order to prevent the carrying out of alterations without consent.

The local authority for your area has many powers and we will be referring to these regularly in each chapter of this guide.

Leasehold

If a person lives in a property owned by someone else and has a written agreement allowing them to occupy the flat or house for a period of time i.e., giving them permission to live in that property, then they will, in the main, have a lease and either be a leaseholder or a tenant of a landlord.

The main principle of a lease is that a person has been given permission by someone else to live in his or her property for a period of time. The person giving permission could be either the freeholder or another leaseholder.

The tenancy agreement is one type of lease. If you have issued a tenancy agreement then you will have given permission to a person to live in your property for a period of time.

The position of the tenant

The tenant will usually have an agreement for a shorter period of time than the typical leaseholder. Whereas the leaseholder will, for example, have an agreement for ninety-nine years, the tenant will have an agreement, which either runs from week to week or month to month (periodic tenancy) or is for a fixed term, for example, six months. These arrangements are the most common types of agreement between the private landlord and tenant, with the six month assured shorthold being the usual tenancy offered by private landlords.

See appendix for a sample tenancy agreement and notices.

The assured tenant

all tenancies, with the exceptions detailed, entered into after 15th January 1989, are known as assured tenancies. An a**ssured shorthold tenancy**, which is the most common form of tenancy used by the landlord nowadays, is one type of assured tenancy, and is for a fixed term of six months minimum and can be brought to an end with two months notice by serving a section 21 (of the Housing Act 1988) notice.

Assured tenancies are governed by the 1988 Housing Act, as amended by the 1996 Housing Act. It is to these Acts, or outlines of the Acts that the landlord must refer when intending to sign a tenancy and let a residential property.

For a tenancy to be assured, three conditions must be fulfilled:

1. The premises must be a dwelling house. This basically means any premises, which can be lived in. Business premises will normally fall outside this interpretation.
2. There must exist a particular relationship between landlord and tenant. In other words there must exist a tenancy agreement. For example, a licence to occupy, as in the case of students, or accommodation occupied as a result of work, cannot be seen as a tenancy. Following on from this, the accommodation must be let as a single unit. The tenant, who must be an individual, must normally be able to sleep, cook and eat in the accommodation. Sharing of bathroom facilities will not prevent a tenancy being an assured tenancy but shared cooking or other facilities, such as a living room, will.
3. The third requirement for an assured tenancy is that the tenant must occupy the dwelling as his or her only or principal home. In situations involving joint tenants at least one of them must occupy.

Tenancies that are not assured

A tenancy agreement will not be assured if one of the following conditions applies:

- The tenancy or the contract was entered into before 15th January 1989.
- If no rent is payable or if only a low rent amounting to less than two thirds of the present ratable value of the property is payable.
- If the premises are let for business purposes or for mixed residential and business purposes.
- If part of the dwelling house is licensed for the sale of liquor for consumption on the premises. This does not include the publican who lets out a flat.
- If the dwelling house is let with more than two acres of agricultural land.
- If the dwelling house is part of an agricultural holding and is occupied in relation to carrying out work on the holding.
- If the premises are let by a specified institution to students, i.e., halls of residence.
- If the premises are let for the purpose of a holiday.
- Where there is a resident landlord, e.g., in the case where the landlord has let one of his rooms but continues to live in the house.
- If the landlord is the Crown (the monarchy) or a government department. Certain lettings by the Crown are capable of being assured, such as some lettings by the Crown Estate Commissioners.
- If the landlord is a local authority, a fully mutual housing association (this is where you have to be a shareholder to be a tenant) of a newly created Housing Action Trust or any similar body listed in the 1988 Housing Act.
- If the letting is transitional such as a tenancy continuing in its original form until phased out, such as a protected tenancy under the 1977 Rent Act.

- Secure tenancy granted before 15th January 1989, e.g., from a local authority or housing association. These tenancies are governed by the 1985 Housing Act).

The Assured Shorthold tenancy

The assured shorthold tenancy as we have seen, is the most common form of tenancy used in the private sector. The main principle of the assured shorthold tenancy is that it is issued for a period of six months minimum and can be brought to an end by the landlord serving two months notice on the tenant. At the end of the six-month period the tenant, if given two months prior notice, by the landlord serving a section 21 notice (see appendix) must leave.

It is important to note that the Deregulation Act, which is due to come into effect from 1 October 2015, states that tenants are always given at least 2 months notice before they have to move out of the property. This prevents a Landlord from serving a Section 21 notice at the start of the tenancy and the tenant being left with having to move out of the Property with little notice at the end of the tenancy. The Act provides that the Section 21 Notice cannot be served until the tenant has lived in the property for a minimum of 4 months. A Section 21 notice will only effectively be able to be served on the Tenant on the first day of month 5 of a Tenancy Agreement.

The section 21 notice, so called because it arises out of Section 21 of the 1988 Housing Act, is the pro-forma that all landlords must use when ending a tenancy.

In addition, The Deregulation Act 2015 introduces a new provision relating to 'retaliatory evictions'. This covers the situation where a tenant might, for example, have complained about the condition of the property to the landlord, as a result of which the landlord might have simply issued a Section 21 Notice to recover possession rather than meet its repairing obligations.

Under the Deregulation Act, where a tenant has a legitimate complaint about the condition of the property before a Section 21 notice is given, and the local authority have issued an enforcement notice requiring the Landlord to improve the condition of the Property, the Section 21 notice is invalid. In practice of course it could take some time for the local authority to inspect the property and provide the enforcement notice. In addition, this provision will only apply to AST's granted on or after 1 October 2015 and will not apply to a fixed term ASTs. It will however will apply to any AST in existence after the end of a period of three years.

A further key change of the Deregulation Act is the introduction of a potential rent refund on the expiry of a Section 21 Notice. This is due to become effective from 1 October 2015 onwards. In practical terms this means that if the Section 21 Notice ends the tenancy at any other time than at the end of a period of a tenancy, and the tenant has moved out, any rent for that period that has been paid in advance may be refunded. The amount to be refunded will be the rent paid for any period where the tenant ceases to live in the property, i.e. any overpaid rent from the expiry of the notice until the next rent payment date.

These provisions are not intended to operate retrospectively and will only apply to new tenancies created after the date that the Deregulation Act came into effect, although changes relating to the protection of tenant's deposits are already effective.

Any property let on an assured tenancy can be let on an assured shorthold, providing the following conditions are met:

- The tenancy must be for a fixed term of not less than six months.
- The agreement cannot contain powers, which enable the landlord to end the tenancy before six months. This does not include the right of the landlord to enforce the grounds for possession, which will be approximately the same as those for the assured tenancy (see below).

- A notice requiring possession at the end of the term is usually served two months before.
- A notice must be served before any rent increase giving one month's clear notice and providing details of the rent increase.

Getting possession of your property before the end of the tenancy

If the landlord wishes to get possession of his/her property, in this case before the expiry of the contractual term, the landlord has to gain a court order.

A notice of seeking possession must be served, giving fourteen days notice and following similar grounds of possession as an assured tenancy (see below).

The landlord cannot simply tell a tenant to leave before the end of the agreed term. A copy of a notice of seeking possession for an assured (shorthold) tenancy is shown in the Appendix.

Tenancy running on after fixed term

An assured shorthold tenancy will become periodic (will run from week to week) when the initial term of six months has elapsed and the landlord has not brought the tenancy to an end. If the tenancy runs on after the end of the fixed term then the landlord can regain possession by giving the required two months notice, as mentioned above. At the end of the term for which the assured shorthold tenancy has been granted, the landlord has an automatic right to possession.

Joint tenancies: the position of two or more people who have a tenancy agreement for one property

Although it is the normal state of affairs for a tenancy agreement to be granted to one person, this is not always the case.

A tenancy can also be granted to two or more people and is then known as a joint tenancy. The position of joint tenants is exactly the same as that of single tenants.

In other words, there is still one tenancy even though it is shared. Each tenant is responsible for paying the rent and observing the terms and conditions of the tenancy agreement. No one joint tenant can prevent another joint tenant's access to the premises. If one of the joint tenants dies then his or her interest will automatically pass to the remaining joint tenants. A joint tenant cannot dispose of his or her interest in a will.

If one joint tenant, however, serves a notice to quit (notice to leave the property) on another joint tenant(s) then the tenancy will come to an end and the landlord can apply to court for a possession order, if the remaining tenant does not leave. The position of a wife or husband in relation to joint tenancies is rather more complex because the married person has more rights when it comes to the home than the single person. Remember, the position of a tenant who has signed a joint tenancy agreement is exactly the same as that of the single tenant.

If one person leaves, the other(s) have the responsibilities of the tenancy. If one person leaves without paying his share of the rent then the other tenants will have to pay instead.

Evicting assured shorthold tenants

As discussed, it is possible to gain possession of a property before the end of the fixed term if the tenancy has been seriously breached. See the chapter on regaining possession of a property. Assured shorthold tenants can be evicted only on certain grounds some discretionary, some mandatory (see below).

In order for the landlord of an assured shorthold tenant to regain possession of the property, using grounds for possession such as non-payment of rent, a notice of seeking possession (of property) must be served, giving fourteen days notice of expiry and stating the ground for possession. Following the fourteen days a court order must be obtained. Although gaining a court order is not complicated, a solicitor will usually be used. Court costs can be awarded against the tenant.

Security of tenure:

There are a number of circumstances called grounds (mandatory and discretionary) whereby a landlord can start a court action to evict a tenant. The following are the mandatory grounds (where the judge must give the landlord possession) and discretionary grounds (where the judge does not have to give the landlord possession) on which a court can order possession if the home is subject to an assured tenancy.

The mandatory grounds for possession

There are eight mandatory grounds for possession, which, if proved, leave the court with no choice but to make an order for possession. It is very important that you understand these.

- *Ground One* is used where the landlord has served a notice, no later than at the beginning of the tenancy, warning the tenant that this ground may be used against him/her.

  This ground is used where the landlord wishes to recover the property as his or her principal (first and only) home or the spouse's (wife's or husbands) principal home. The ground is not available to a person who bought the premises for gain (profit) whilst they were occupied.
- *Ground Two* is available where the property is subject to a mortgage and if the landlord does not pay the mortgage, could lose the home.
- *Grounds Three and Four* relate to holiday lettings.
- *Ground Five* is a special one, applicable to ministers of religion.
- *Ground Six* relates to the demolition or reconstruction of the property.
- *Ground Seven* applies if a tenant dies and in his will leaves the tenancy to someone else: but the landlord must start proceedings against the new tenant within a year of the death if he wants to evict the new tenant.
- *Ground Eight* concerns rent arrears. This ground applies if, both at the date of the serving of the notice seeking possession and at the date of the hearing of the action, the rent is at least 8 weeks in arrears or two months in arrears.

This is the main ground used by landlords when rent is not being paid.

One of the advantages of a court order is that you will have details of the tenant's employers and can get an attachment of earnings against the tenant.

The discretionary grounds for possession of a property

As we have seen, the discretionary grounds for possession are those in relation to which the court has some powers over whether or not the landlord can evict. In other words, the final decision is left to the judge.

- *Ground Nine* applies when suitable alternative accommodation is available or will be when the possession order takes effect. As we have seen, if the landlord wishes to obtain possession of his or her property in order to use it for other purposes then suitable alternative accommodation has to be provided.
- *Ground Ten* deals with rent arrears as does ground eleven. These grounds are distinct from the mandatory grounds, as there does not have to be a fixed arrear in terms of time scale, e.g., 8 weeks. The judge, therefore, has some choice as to whether or not to evict. In practice, this ground will not be relevant to managers of assured shorthold tenancies.
- *Ground Twelve* concerns any broken obligation of the tenancy. As we have seen with the protected tenancy, there are a number of conditions of the tenancy agreement, such as the requirement not to racially or sexually harass a neighbour. Ground Twelve will be used if these conditions are broken.
- *Ground Thirteen* deals with the deterioration of the dwelling as a result of a tenant's neglect. This is connected with the structure of the property and is the same as for a protected tenancy. It puts the responsibility on the tenant to look after the premises.

- *Ground Fourteen* concerns nuisance, annoyance and illegal or immoral use. This is where a tenant or anyone connected with the tenant has caused a nuisance to neighbours.
- *Ground Fourteen A* this ground deals with domestic violence.
- *Ground Fifteen* concerns the condition of the furniture and neglect.

The description of the grounds above is intended as a guide only. For a fuller description please refer to the 1988 Housing Act, section 7, Schedule two,) as amended by the 1996 Housing Act) which is available at reference libraries. As we have discussed, it is usual for the landlord of an assured shorthold tenancy to serve a notice requiring possession on the tenant giving two months notice.

It is unusual for a landlord to take an assured shorthold tenant to court on one of the grounds for possession. However, these circumstances do arise, where a tenant has breached the tenancy very early on and the landlord cannot wait for the fixed term to expire.

Fast track possession

In November 1993, following changes to the County Court Rules, a facility was introduced which enables landlords of tenants with assured shorthold tenancies to apply for possession of their property without the usual time delay involved in waiting for a court date and attendance at court. This is known as "fast track possession" It cannot be used for rent arrears or other grounds. It is used to gain possession of a property when the fixed term of six months or more has come to an end, a valid section 21 notice has been served and the tenant will not move.

The contract between landlord and tenant

Typically, any tenancy agreement will show the name and address of the landlord and will state the names of the tenant(s). The type of tenancy agreement that is signed should be clearly indicated.

In the main, the agreement will be an assured shorthold tenancy. The date the tenancy began and the duration (fixed term or periodic) plus the amount of rent payable should be clearly shown along with who is responsible for any other charges, such as water rates, council tax etc, and a description of the property you are renting out. In addition to the rent that must be paid there should be a clear indication of when a rent increase can be expected.

This information is sometimes shown in other conditions of tenancy, which should be given to the tenant when they move into their home. The conditions of tenancy will set out landlords and tenants rights and obligations.

If services are provided, i.e., if a service charge is payable, this should be indicated in the agreement. The tenancy agreement should indicate clearly the address to which notices on the landlord can be served by the tenant, for example, because of repair problems or notice of leaving the property. The landlord has a legal requirement to indicate this.

The tenancy agreement will either be a basic document with the above information or will be more comprehensive. Either way, there will be a section beginning "the tenant agrees."

Here the tenant will agree to move into the property, pay rent, use the property as an only home, not cause a nuisance to others, take responsibility for certain internal repairs, not sublet the property, i.e., create another tenancy, and various other things depending on the property. There should also be another section "the landlord agrees". Here, the landlord is contracting with the tenant to allow quiet enjoyment of the property. The landlord's repairing responsibilities are also usually outlined.

Finally, there should be a section entitled "ending the tenancy" which will outline the ways in which landlord and tenant can end the agreement. It is in this section that the landlord should make reference to the "grounds for possession". Grounds for possession are circumstances where the landlord will apply to court for possession of his/her property.

Some of these grounds relate to what is in the tenancy, i.e., the responsibility to pay rent and to not cause a nuisance.

Other grounds do not relate to the contents of the tenancy directly, but more to the law governing that particular tenancy. The grounds for possession are very important, as they are used in any court case brought against the tenant. Unfortunately, they are not always indicated in the tenancy agreement. As they are so important they are summarized later on in this chapter.

The responsibility of the landlord to provide a rent book

As most tenancies nowadays are fixed term assured shortholds then it is not strictly necessary to provide a tenant with a rent book. However, for the purposes of business efficiency, and your own records, it is always useful to issue a rent book to tenants and sign it.

Overcrowding and the rules governing too many people living in the property

It is important to understand, when signing a tenancy agreement, that it is not permitted to allow the premises to become overcrowded, i.e., to allow more people than was originally intended, (which is outlined in the agreement) to live in the property. If a tenant does then the landlord can take action to evict.

Other types of agreement

In addition to the assured shorthold tenancy agreements there are other types of agreement sometimes used in privately rented property. One of these is the company let, as we discussed in chapter five, and another is the license agreement. The person signing such an agreement is called a licensee. Licenses will only apply in special circumstances where the licensee cannot be given sole occupation of his home and therefore can only stay for a short period with minimum rights.

The right to quiet enjoyment of a property

Earlier, we saw that when a tenancy agreement is signed, the landlord is contracting to give quiet enjoyment of the tenants home. This means that they have the right to live peacefully in the home without harassment. The landlord is obliged not to do anything that will disturb the right to the quiet enjoyment of the home. The most serious breach of this right would be for the landlord to wrongfully evict a tenant.

Now read the main points from chapter seven overleaf

****

Main points from chapter seven

- **Private Tenant**. A tenant of a landlord who is not a public landlord, public landlord being for example a local authority or housing association. The most common private tenancy relationship is between two individuals or between an individual and a company.
- **Leasehold and freehold**. These are the two main types of ownership of land and occupation of property. A freeholder will own the property outright (usually with a mortgage). A leaseholder has the right to live there for a period of time.
- **Tenancy agreement**. The tenancy agreement is one form of lease. It is a contract between the landlord and tenant for the occupation of property. The tenancy agreement is either for a specific length (e.g., six months) of time or from week to week or month to month. The agreement will govern the length of notice given by the landlord or tenant when requiring the property back, or in the case of the tenant, leaving the property.
- **Rent book**. If a tenancy is a weekly periodic tenancy, then a landlord must provide a tenant with a rent book.
- **Overcrowding**. A tenant must not allow his/her home to become overcrowded. A landlord can take a tenant to court and can evict in this case.
- **The assured tenant**. This is the usual type of tenancy agreement entered into after 15th January 1989, which is regulated by the 1988 Housing Act (as amended). In chapter eight we discuss this type of agreement.
- **Quiet enjoyment**. A tenant has the right to quiet enjoyment of his/her home.
- **Eviction**. It is a criminal offence to unlawfully evict a tenant from his or her home.

Chapter 8

Understanding Rent and The Sources of Rent

As must have become apparent by now, rent is the key to your survival as a residential landlord, It is vital to understand the issues surrounding rent and the payment of rent, in particular the various sources of rent, including housing benefit.

The assured tenant

The assured (shorthold) tenant has far fewer rights in relation to rent control than the protected tenant.

The Housing Act 1988 allows a landlord to charge whatever he likes. There is no right to a fair or reasonable rent with an assured tenancy, which at this moment in time is very high, particularly in London. The rent can sometimes be negotiated at the outset of the tenancy. This rent has to be paid as long as the contractual term of the tenancy lasts. Once the contractual term has expired, the landlord is entitled to continue to charge the same rent.

On expiry of an assured shorthold the landlord is free to grant a new tenancy and set the rent to a level that is compatible with the market.

Rent control for assured shorthold tenants

We have seen that the assured shorthold tenancy is for a period of six months minimum. Like the assured tenant, the assured shorthold tenant has no right to request that a fair rent should be set. The rent is a market rent. As with an assured tenancy, the assured shorthold tenant has the right to appeal to a Rent Assessment Committee in the case of what he/she considers an unreasonable rent.

This may be done during the contractual term. The Committee will consider whether the rent is significantly higher than is usual for a similar property. If the Committee assesses a different rent from that set by the landlord, they may set a date when the increase will take effect. The rent cannot be backdated to before the date of the application. Once a decision has been reached by the Committee, the landlord cannot increase the rent for at least twelve months, or on termination of the tenancy.

Local housing allowance (LHA) (housing benefit) for people who rent a home from a private landlord.

Local housing allowance is housing benefit for private sector tenants. It's usually paid directly to the tenant and they pay their landlord. Local housing allowance is housing benefit that helps pay the rent and some service charges (if applicable) if a person rents from a private landlord. It's a benefit administered by the local council. LHA has many of the same rules as housing benefit, but there are some extra rules that limit the amount of help a tenant can get for a private rented home.

Claim LHA

A person can claim local housing allowance if they are a private tenant who needs help with paying the rent. They may be entitled to this housing benefit if they are working or if they claim benefits.

A person can't get LHA if they have savings of £16,000 or more unless they are a pensioner and receive the guarantee credit part of pension credit. An LHA claim is routinely reassessed after 12 months. The claim may be reassessed at any time if circumstances change.

It is worth noting that, in the July 2015 budget, it was stated that people between the ages of 18-21 will not be entitled to housing benefit in the future. This change has yet to come into effect but you should check with your local authority of you have a prospective tenant between these ages.

How LHA is calculated

The amount of LHA a person can get depends on their income and savings and if any non-dependants live with them, for example adult children.

The amount of LHA they receive also depends on the maximum rent allowed for properties in the area and the number of rooms the council decides a person need.

A person can rent a home of any size or price, but theirr housing benefit claim is limited. You have to make up any rent shortfall.

Maximum LHA amounts

There are limits on the amount of LHA a person can get. The maximum weekly LHA rate limits are:

£260.64 for a room in shared accommodation
£260.64 for 1 bedroom accommodation
£302.33 for 2 bedroom accommodation
£354.46 for 3 bedroom accommodation
£417.02 for 4 bedroom accommodation

The amount of LHA a person may be eligible for depends on where they live. Local limits are based on the cheapest 30% of properties in an area.

Rooms allowed when calculating LHA

A person is assessed as needing a bedroom for the following people in their home:

- an adult couple
- another person aged 16 or over
- any two children of the same sex up to the age of 16
- any two children regardless of sex under the age of 10
- any other child

An extra bedroom can be allowed if they:

- have a foster child or children
- have a severely disabled child who needs their own room
- or their partner is disabled and a carer provides regular overnight care
- have a child who is away on duty with the armed forces and intends to return home
- A person cannot be allowed more than four bedrooms for the purposes of calculating LHA.

If aged under 35

A Person is usually only entitled to LHA at the reduced shared accommodation rate if they are a single person under age 35 without children or they live in shared accommodation.

How often is housing benefit paid?

Payment of housing benefit depends on how often rent is paid. Housing benefit is not paid in advance. Each payment covers a past period.

When LHA can be paid direct to landlords

Your council must make a tenant's LHA payments direct to their landlord if:

- they have rent arrears of eight weeks or more
- deductions are being made from benefits for rent arrears
- In some cases, the council can choose to pay LHA direct to the landlord. They could do this if the tenant has failed to pay the rent in the past or have had problems paying rent because of a medical condition. The council can pay LHA direct to a landlord if this will help the tenant keep their tenancy.

If a person has support needs, the council can pay LHA to the landlord to encourage them to keep a person as a tenant.

The council will consult the tenant and people supporting them before deciding to pay LHA direct to the landlord. This may include their doctor, support worker, probation officer and others who know about their situation.

Council tax and the tenant

Council tax is based on properties, or dwellings, and not individual people.

This means that there is one bill for each individual dwelling, rather than separate bills for each person. The number and type of people who live in the dwelling may affect the size of the final bill. A discount of 25 percent is given for people who live alone. Each property is placed in a valuation band with different properties paying more or less depending on their individual value. Tenants who feel that their home has been placed in the wrong valuation band can appeal to their local authority council tax department.

Who has to pay the council tax?

In most cases the tenant occupying the dwelling will have to pay the council tax. That person is known as the 'liable person'. Nobody under the age of 18 can be a liable person.

Couples living together will both be liable even if there is only one name appearing on the bill. However, a landlord will be responsible for paying the council tax where:

- there are several households living in one dwelling where households pay rent separately or;
- where people are under the age of 18;
- the people who live in the property are all asylum seekers who are not entitled to claim benefits including council tax benefits;
- the people who are staying in the property are there temporarily
- or the property is a care home/hospital/hostel or women's refuge.

Although the landlord has the responsibility for paying the council tax, he or she will normally try to pass on the increased cost through rents. However, there is a set procedure for a landlord to follow if he/she wishes to increase rent.

The rules covering council tax liability can be obtained from a Citizens Advice Bureau or from your local authority council tax department.

Service charges-What is a service charge?

A service charge covers a provision of services other than those covered by the rent. In practice, a leaseholder sub-letting his flat will also have to take into account service charges. A rental payment will normally cover maintenance charges, loan charges if any, and also profit. Other services, such as cleaning and gardening, will be covered by a separate charge, known as a service charge. A registered rent reflects the cost of any services provided by the landlord. An assured rent set by a landlord will normally include services which must be outlined in the agreement. The fact that the charges are variable must be written into a tenancy agreement and the landlord has a legal duty to provide the tenant with annual budgets and accounts and has to consult when he or She wishes to spend over a certain amount of money, currently £250 per dwelling for major works such as decorating or £100 if renewing a contract such as gardening, cleaning or lift maintenance, per scheme (estate or block of flats), whichever is the greater.

The form of consultation, which must take place, is that of writing to all those affected informing them of:

- The landlord's intention to carry out work (30 days notice).
- Why these works are seen to be necessary.
- The estimated cost of the works (further 30 days notice).
- At least two estimates or the inviting of them to see two estimates.

The landlord can incur reasonable expense, without consultation, if the work is deemed to be necessary, i.e. emergency works. If a service charge is variable then a landlord has certain legal obligations, which are clearly laid out in the 1985 and 1987 Landlord and Tenant Acts as amended by the 1996 Housing Act and the 2002 Commonhold and Leasehold Reform Act. If you intend to let property for profit then it is of the utmost importance that you understand the law governing service charges.

Payment of housing benefit directly to the landlord

Housing benefit is a payment made to the tenant rather than the landlord. The amount of benefit that a tenant is paid will very much depend on that persons circumstances. The rules regarding payment of housing benefit have tightened considerably over the years and if you know that a tenant is going to be claiming housing benefit then you should be sure that they will be entitled. Local authorities have local rents that they will pay and they will not pay, for example, for a single person to occupy accommodation surplus to their needs or for anyone to claim what they see as excessive rent.

New benefit rules which came into effect in April 2013 impose a 'bedroom tax' on tenants and tenants will receive reductions for every bedroom above their needs. Landlords should be aware of these changes as they are a possible cause of arrears. In addition, there were changes to council tax benefit from April 2013 which resulted in a reduction in this benefit to many tenants. Essentially, council tax benefit has been abolished, with local authorities being given an allowance, which invariably is not enough to cover the existing subsidies.

Finally, watch out for the introduction of Universal Credit which is still rumbling along but which transforms the payments of benefits to those who are in receipt of welfare benefits and which could pose yet further problems for landlords.

Housing benefit and possession for arrears of rent

Very often, problems in obtaining benefit will cause tenants to accrue rent arrears. The court is unlikely to give possession if arrears are accruing because of benefit.

Once there are eight weeks of arrears (see grounds for possession) then the court has no choice but to give possession anyway and quite often it is better to wait rather than jumping the gun and losing rental income altogether. If on the other hand the tenant has stated that they are going to pay rent personally rather than benefit then the court will look more favorably on- giving possession to the landlord if arrears have arisen as a result of an immediate claim for benefit.

Now read the main points from chapter eight overleaf.

****

Main points from chapter eight

- **Putting the rent up**. Even if the fair rent is higher than the existing rent, the landlord cannot charge more until the expiry of the two-year period.
- **Assured tenancies**. If a tenancy is assured there will not be the protection of the 1977 Rent Act and no entitlement to a fair rent. The rent charged would be a market rent.
- **Council tax**. If the tenant does not receive an individual bill for council tax then the landlord will be responsible for payment. This is usually the case in a multi-occupied home or block. The landlord cannot increase the rent without either notifying the Rent Officer or giving the required notice if an assured tenant.
- **Service charge**. A service charge is a charge for services such as cleaning or gardening. A landlord must show the cost of services clearly unless the total charge is less than 5 percent of rent. The service charge can be variable, e.g., varied once a year, or fixed, where it cannot be increased until the end of the two-year period.
- Watch out for benefit changes which took place in 2013 which could potentially cause arrears.

****

Chapter 9

Landlord and Tenant Repairing Rights and Obligations

Repairs and improvements generally: The landlord and tenants obligations

Repairs are essential works to keep the property in good order. Improvements and alterations to the property, e.g. the installation of a shower.

As we have seen, most tenancies are periodic, i.e. week-to-week or month-to-month. If a tenancy falls into this category, or is a fixed-term tenancy for less than seven years, and began after October 1961, then a landlord is legally responsible for most major repairs to the flat or house.

If a tenancy began after 15th January 1989 then, in addition to the above responsibility, the landlord is also responsible for repairs to common parts and service fittings.

The area of law dealing with the landlord and tenants repairing obligations is the 1985 Landlord and Tenant Act, section 11.

This section of the Act is known as a covenant and cannot be excluded by informal agreement between landlord and tenant. In other words the landlord is legally responsible whether he or she likes it or not. Parties to a tenancy, however, may make an application to a court mutually to vary or exclude this section.

Example of repairs a landlord is responsible for:

- Leaking roofs and guttering.
- Rotting windows.
- Rising damp.
- Damp walls.

- Faulty electrical wiring.
- Dangerous ceilings and staircases.
- Faulty gas and water pipes.
- Broken water heaters and boilers.
- Broken lavatories, sinks or baths.

In shared housing the landlord must see that shared halls, stairways, kitchens and bathrooms are maintained and kept clean and lit.

Normally, tenants are responsible only for minor repairs, e.g., broken door handles, cupboard doors, etc. Tenants will also be responsible for decorations unless they have been damaged as a result of the landlord's failure to do repair.

A landlord will be responsible for repairs only if the repair has been reported. It is therefore important to report repairs in writing and keep a copy. If the repair is not carried out then action can be taken. Damages can also be claimed.

Compensation can be claimed, with the appropriate amount being the reduction in the value of the premises to the tenant caused by the landlord's failure to repair. If the tenant carries out the repairs then the amount expended will represent the decrease in value.

The tenant does not have the right to withhold rent because of a breach of repairing covenant by the landlord. However, depending on the repair, the landlord will not have a very strong case in court if rent is withheld.

Reporting repairs to landlords

The tenant has to tell the landlord or the person collecting the rent straight away when a repair needs doing. It is advisable that it is in writing, listing the repairs that need to be done.

Once a tenant has reported a repair the landlord must do it within a reasonable period of time. What is reasonable will depend on the nature of the repair.

The tenants rights whilst repairs are being carried out

The landlord must ensure that the repairs are done in an orderly and efficient way with minimum inconvenience to the tenant If the works are disruptive or if property or decorations are damaged the tenant can apply to the court for compensation or, if necessary, for an order to make the landlord behave reasonably.

If the landlord genuinely needs the house empty to do the work he/she can ask the tenant to vacate it and can if necessary get a court order against the tenant.

A written agreement should be drawn up making it clear that the tenant can move back in when the repairs are completed and stating what the arrangements for fuel charges and rent are.

Can the landlord put the rent up after doing repairs?

If there is a service charge for maintenance, the landlord may be able to pass on the cost of the work(s).

Tenants rights to make improvements to a property

Unlike carrying out repairs the tenant will not normally have the right to insist that the landlord make actual alterations to the home. However, a tenant needs the following amenities and the law states that you should have:

- Bath or shower.
- Wash hand basin.
- Hot and cold water at each bath, basin or shower.
- An indoor toilet.

If these amenities do not exist then the tenant can contact the council's Environmental Health Officer. An improvement notice can be served on the landlord ordering him to put the amenity in.

Disabled tenants

If a tenant is disabled he/she may need special items of equipment in the accommodation. The local authority may help in providing and, occasionally, paying for these. The tenant will need to obtain the permission of the landlord. If you require more information then contact the social services department locally.

Shared housing. The position of tenants in shared houses (Houses in Multiple Occupation)

A major change to improve standards of shared housing was introduced in 2006. The parts of the Housing Act 2004 relating to the licensing of HMO's (Houses in Multiple Occupation) and the new Health and Safety Rating System for assessing property conditions came into effect on 6rh April 2006.

The Act requires landlords of many HMO's to apply for licences. The HMO's that need to be licensed are those with:

- Three or more storeys, which are
- Occupied by five or more people forming two or more households (i.e. people not related, living together as a couple etc) and
- Which have an element of shared facilities (eg kitchen, bathroom etc)

As far as licensing is concerned, attics and basements are included as storeys if they are used as living accommodation. Previously, HMO's were only defined as houses converted into flats or bedsits, but the new Act widens this definition and many more types of shared houses are now included.

A local authority will have a list of designated properties will have a list of those properties which are designated HMO's and they will need to be licensed.

Usually, landlords will need to apply to a local authority private sector unit for licences. It is illegal for landlords to manage designated properties without a licence since July 2006. Landlords will have to complete an application form and pay a fee, the local authority will then assess whether the property is suitable for the number of people the landlord wants to rent it to. In most case, the local authority, their agents, will visit a property to assess facilities and also fire precautions. A decision will then be taken to grant a license. There is a fee for registration, councils set the fee and the ones shown below are indicative of a southern local authority:

- Shared houses-five sharers landlords first house £640
- Subsequent house £590
- Plus £10 each additional occupier over five

Hostels

- 10 occupiers £690
- 20 occupiers £790
- 50 occupiers £1100
- 75 occupiers £1340

The landlord of a HMO has certain duties under the regulations to his/her tenants:

Duty to provide information

The manager (this means that whoever is charged with the management of the building) must ensure that:

- His name, address and telephone number are available to each household in the HMO
- These details are also clearly displayed in a prominent position in the HMO.

The manager should maintain a log book to record all events at the property such as:

- Testing of fire alarms
- Testing of fire fighting equipment
- Gas safety certificate
- Electrical report
- Inspection and wants of repair

Duty to take safety measures

The manager must ensure that all means of escape from fire in the property are kept free from obstruction and in good order as should all fire alarms and equipment.

The manager should ensure that the structure is designed and maintained in a safe condition, and also take steps to protect occupiers from injury. In properties with four or more occupants, the Regulations provide that fire escape notices be clearly displayed.

Duty to maintain water supply drainage

The manager must ensure that the water supply and drainage system serving the property are maintained in a good working condition. More specifically, water fittings should be protected from frost and all water storage tanks should be provided with covers.

Duty to supply and maintain gas and electricity

The manager must supply the local housing authority within 7 days of receiving a written request a safety certificate. The manager must ensure that the fixed electrical installation is checked at least once every three years by a suitably qualified electrician and supply this to the LHA on written request. In addition to the above, there is a duty to maintain common parts, fixtures, fittings and appliances. There is a duty to maintain living accommodation and to provide waste disposal facilities.

Powers of the local authority in relation to HMO's

It is essential to ensure that, if you have invested in a HMO that you manage it rigorously because local authorities have sweeping powers to fine landlords and to revoke licenses. A local authority can prosecute a landlord who does not obtain a license for a HMO.

Safety generally for all landlords-the regulations

The main product safety regulations relevant to the lettings industry are:

Gas safety

The Gas safety (Installation and use) Regulations 1998
The Gas Cooking Appliances (safety) Regulations 1989
Heating Appliances(Fireguard) (safety) Regulations 1991
Gas Appliances(Safety) Regulations 1995

All of the above are based on the fact that the supply of gas and the appliances in a dwelling are safe. A Gas Safety certificate is required to validate this.

Furniture Safety

Furniture and Furnishings (Fire) (Safety) Regulations 1988 and 1993 (as amended). Landlords and lettings agents are included in these regulations. The regulations set high standards for fire resistance for domestic upholstered furniture and other products containing upholstery.

The main provisions are:

- Upholstered articles (i.e. beds, sofas, armchairs etc) must have fire resistant filling material.
- Upholstered articles must have passed a match resistant test or, if of certain kinds (such as cotton or silk) be used with a fire resistant interliner.

- The combination of the cover fabric and the filling material must have passed a cigarette resistance test.

The landlord should inspect property for non-compliant items before letting and replace with compliant items.

Electrical Safety

Electrical Equipment (Safety) Regulations 1994
Plugs and Sockets etc. (Safety) Regulations 1994.

The Electrical Equipment Regulations came into force in January 1995. Both sets of regulations relate to the supply of electrical equipment designed with a working voltage of between 50 and 1000 volts ac. (or between 75 and 1000 volts dc.) the regulations cover all the mains voltage household electrical goods including cookers, kettles, toasters, electric blankets, washing machines, immersion heaters etc. The regulations do not apply to items attached to land. This is generally considered to exclude the fixed wiring and built in appliances (e.g. central heating systems) from the regulations. Lettings agents and landlords should take the following action:

Essential:

Check all electrical appliances in all managed properties on a regular fixed term basis. Remove unsafe items and keep a record of checks.

Recommended:

- Have appliances checked by a qualified electrical engineer
- Avoid purchasing second hand electrical items
- There is no specific requirement for regular testing under the regulations. However, it is recommended that a schedule of checks, say on an annual basis, is put in place.

The availability of grants

There are a number of grants available to landlords at any one time which will enable improvements to take place to a property. One of the main grants is the Disabled facilities Grant. However, there are more and your local authority can tell you what is available.

New regulations on Smoke and Carbon Monoxide detectors

From October 2015, all landlords, regardless of whether public or private sector, will be required to install working smoke and carbon monoxide alarms in their properties, on each floor. The carbon monoxide alarms will need to be placed in high risk areas, i.e., where there are gas appliances such as boilers or fires. Carbon monoxide detectors will not be required in properties where there are no gas or solid fuel appliances. A civil penalty of up to £5,000 will apply to landlords who fail to comply with this legislation.

Sanitation health and hygiene

Local authorities have a duty to serve an owner with a notice requiring the provision of a WC when a property has insufficient sanitation, sanitation meaning toilet waste disposal.

They will also serve notice if it is thought that the existing sanitation is inadequate and is harmful to health or is a nuisance.

Local authorities have similar powers under various Public Health Acts to require owners to put right bad drains and sewers, also food storage facilities and vermin, plus the containing of disease.

The Environmental Health Department, if it considers the problem bad enough will serve a notice requiring the landlord to put the defect right. In certain cases the local authority can actually do the work and require the landlord to pay for it. This is called work in default.

Now read the main points from Chapter nine overleaf.

Main points from chapter nine

- Responsibility for repairs. If a tenancy is periodic or of a fixed term for less than seven years and began after October 1961, a landlord is legally responsible for certain repairs.
- The law. The landlord has repairing obligations under the Landlord and Tenant Act 1985, section 11.
- Tenants responsibility. Normally, tenants are responsible only for minor internal repairs.
- Landlords responsibility. A landlord will only be responsible for a repair if it has been reported.
- Local authority. If a landlord does not carry out repairs then the local authority in particular the Environmental Health Department can get involved.
- Inconvenience. A tenant has certain rights whilst repairs are being done, particularly for inconvenience.
- Improvements. A tenant will not normally have the right to make improvements. However, they are entitled to certain basic amenities, such as a shower or a bath.
- Disabled. A disabled tenant may need certain items of equipment in their home. The local authority can advise and assist in this area, even helping with payment.
- Shared housing. There are special laws governing housing in multiple occupation (shared housing) particularly in relation to health and safety. The local authority can advise.
- Local authority grants. Private tenants may be entitled to a grant to help with work on a property. The local authority will advise on entitlement.

****

Chapter 10

Taking Back Possession of Your Property After or Before the Tenancy Ends

Fast-track possession

In normal circumstances, the landlord will have served a section 21 notice on the tenant at the start of the tenancy. This brings the tenancy to an end on the day of expiry, i.e. on the day of expiry of the six month period, or 12 month period, whichever is appropriate. It should be noted that if a landlord takes a deposit from the tenant then every deposit must be registered with the appropriate deposit service before the landlord can serve the s21 notice. It should also be noted that if a section 21 notice is served after the end of the fixed term giving two months notice then the notice should be a section 21 (b). This is important as a service of the incorrect notice can delay proceedings.

On expiry of the notice, if it is the landlord's intention to take possession of the property then the tenants should leave. It is worthwhile writing a letter to the tenants one month before expiry reminding them that they should leave.

In the event of the tenant refusing to leave, then the landlord has to then follow a process termed 'fast track possession'. This entails filling in the appropriate forms (N5B) which can be downloaded from Her Majesty's Court Service Website www.justice.gov.uk.

Assuming that a valid section 21 notice has been served on the tenant, the accelerated possession proceedings can begin and the forms completed and lodged with the court dealing with the area where the property is situated. In order to grant the accelerated possession order the court will require the following:

- The assured shorthold agreement
- The section 21 notice
- Evidence of service of the section 21 notice

The best form of service of the s21 notice is by hand. If you have already served the notice then evidence that the tenant has received it will be required.

Having the correct original paperwork is of the utmost importance. Without this, the application will fail and delays will be incurred.

If the tenant disputes the possession proceedings in any way they will have 14 days to reply to the court. If the case is well founded and the paperwork is in order then there should be no case for defence. Once the accelerated possession order has been granted then this will need to be served on the tenant, giving them 14 days to vacate. In certain circumstances, if the tenant pleads hardship the court can grant extra time to leave, six weeks as opposed to two weeks. If they still do not vacate then an application will need to be made to court for a bailiffs warrant to evict the tenants.

Accelerated possession proceedings cannot be used against the tenant for rent arrears. It will be necessary to follow the procedure below.

An accelerated possession order remains in force for six years from the date it was granted.

Going to court to end the tenancy

There may come a time when you need to go to court to regain possession of your property. This will usually arise when the contract has been breached by the tenant, for non-payment of rent or for some other breach such as nuisance or harassment. As we have seen, a tenancy can be brought to an end in a court on one of the grounds for possession. However, as the tenancy will usually be an assured shorthold then it is necessary to consider whether you are in a position to give two months notice and withhold the deposit, as opposed to going to court. The act of withholding the deposit will entail you refusing to authorize the payment to the tenant online. This then brings arbitration into the frame. Deposit schemes have an arbitration system as an integral part of the scheme.

If you decide, for whatever reason, to go to court, then any move to regain your property for breach of agreement will commence in the county court in the area in which the property is. The first steps in ending the tenancy will necessitate the serving of a notice of seeking possession using one of the Grounds for Possession detailed earlier in the book. If the tenancy is protected then 28 days must be given, the notice must be in prescribed form and served on the tenant personally (preferably).

If the tenancy is an assured shorthold, which is more often the case now, then 14 days notice of seeking possession can be used. In all cases the ground to be relied upon must be clearly outlined in the notice. If the case is more complex, then this will entail a particulars of claim being prepared, usually by a solicitor, as opposed to a standard possession form.

A fee is paid when sending the particulars to court, which should be checked with the local county court. The standard form which the landlord uses for routine rent arrears cases is called the N119 and the accompanying summons is called the N5. Both of these forms can be obtained from the court or from www.courtservice.gov. When completed, the forms should be sent in duplicate to the county court and a copy retained for you.

The court will send a copy of the particulars of claim and the summons to the tenant. They will send you a form which gives you a case number and court date to appear, known as the return date. On the return date, you should arrive at court at least 15 minutes early. You can represent yourself in simple cases but are advised to use a solicitor for more contentious cases. When it is your turn to present the case, you should have your file in order, a copy of all relevant notices served and a current rent arrears figure or a copy of the particulars for other cases.

If it is simple rent arrears then quite often the judge will guide you through.

However, the following are the steps to observe:

- State your name and address.
- Tenants name and address.
- Start date of tenancy.
- Current rent and arrears.
- Date notice served-a copy should be produced for the judge.
- Circumstances of tenant (financial and other) this is where you make your case.
- Copy of order wanted.

If the tenant is present then they will have a chance to defend themselves.

A number of orders are available. However, if you have gone to court on the mandatory ground eight then if the fact is proved then you will get possession immediately. If not, then the judge can grant an order, suspended whilst the tenant finds time to pay.

In a lot of cases, it is more expedient for a landlord to serve notice-requiring possession, if the tenancy has reached the end of the period, and then wait two months before the property is regained. This saves the cost and time of going to court particularly if the ground is one of nuisance or other, which will involve solicitors.

In many cases, if you are contemplating going to court and have never been before and do not know the procedure then it is best to use a solicitor to guide the case through.

Costs can be recovered from the tenant, although this will depend on their means. If you regain possession of your property midway through the contractual term then you will have to complete the possession process by use of bailiff, pay a fee and fill in another form, Warrant for Possession of Land.

If you have reached the end of the contractual term and wish to recover your property then a fast track procedure is available which entails gaining an order for possession and bailiff's order by post. This can be used in cases with the exception of rent arrears.

Now read the main points from chapter ten overleaf.

****

Main points from chapter ten

- One of the unpleasant sides of being a landlord is that you may have to go to court to regain possession of a property.

- Any move to regain possession of your property will commence in the local county court where the property is. Fourteen days service of notice is needed and a fee is payable to the court. It is usually best to employ a solicitor to take this action.

- In many cases it is better to serve a section 21 notice and regain possession either at the end of the fixed term or after two months from service rather than incur the expense of court action.

****

Chapter 11

Tenancies in Scotland

The law governing the relationship between private landlords and tenants in Scotland is different to that in England. Since the beginning of 1989, new private sector tenancies in Scotland have been covered by the Housing (Scotland) Act 1988. Following the passage of this Act, private sector tenants no longer have any protection as far as rent levels are concerned and tenants enjoy less security of tenure.

There are four essential elements in the creation of a tenancy under Scottish law:

- An agreement between landlord and tenant.
- The payment of rent. If someone is allowed to occupy a property without an agreement then this will not amount to a tenancy.
- A fixed permission date (called an 'ish').
- Possession.

The agreement must be in writing if the tenancy is for a period of 1 year or more. Agreements of less than a year can be oral.

Different types of tenancy

There are different tenancy types in the private sector, differing according to when they were entered into. In the case of assured tenancies they will differ depending on what landlord and tenant agreed between themselves. The different types of tenancy are:

- Protected tenancy.

- Statutory tenancy.
- Assured tenancy.
- Short assured tenancy.

Protected tenancies

Before 1989, most private sector tenancies were likely to be protected tenancies. A protected tenancy is a contractual tenancy covered by the Rent Act (Scotland) 1984 and must satisfy the following requirements:

- The house must be let as a dwelling house (this can apply to a house or part of a house).
- The house must be a separate dwelling.
- The ratable value must be less than a specified sum.

Various categories of dwellings did not qualify as protected tenancies. A protected tenancy retains its status until the death of a tenant or his spouse, or any eligible successor, and therefore some protected tenancies are still in existence today.

Grounds for possession

As is the case in England and Wales, where there is no protected tenancy, the landlord may possess a property only by obtaining a court order. The landlord must serve a notice to quit, giving 28 days notice. A ground for possession must be shown, either discretionary or mandatory before possession can be given. The grounds for possession are similar to those in England and Wales, with ten mandatory and ten discretionary grounds applying.

Fair rent system

A fair rent system, similar to England and Wales, exists in Scotland for protected tenants.

There is a set procedure to be followed, with either the landlord or tenant, or jointly, making an application to the rent officer. Once fixed, the rent is valid for three years. A fresh application can be made within three years if circumstances relating to the tenancy radically alter, such as a substantial refurbishment.

Statutory tenancies

A statutory tenancy is one which arises when a tenant remains in possession of a house after the contractual tenancy has been terminated (e.g. by a notice to quit) or a tenant has previously succeeded to the tenancy before 1990. A statutory tenant has similar rights to a protected tenant.

Assured tenants

Under the Housing (Scotland) Act 1988, the assured tenancy was introduced into Scotland coming into force after 2nd January 1989. This is very similar indeed to the assured tenancy introduced into England and Wales in 1989.

A Scottish assured tenancy has three elements:

- The tenancy must be of a house or flat or self contained dwelling. For an agreement to exist, there must be an agreement, rent payable, a termination date and possession, as there is in all leases in Scotland.
- The house must be let as a separate dwelling. A tenancy may be of a flat, part of a house, or even a single room, provided it is possible for the tenant to carry on all 'the major activities of residential life there, i.e. sleeping, cooking and feeding.
- The tenant must be an individual. A company cannot be given an assured tenancy.

The list of exclusions from assured tenancy status are the same as those in England and all the other provisions concerning rent, sub-letting succession, security of tenure and so on, apply. The grounds for possession and the law governing termination of tenancies is a reflection of English Law.

Short-assured tenancies

The Housing Act (Scotland) also introduced 'short assured tenancies', a distinct form of assured tenancy for a fixed term of six months. Again, this is a reflection of the assured shorthold with the same provisions applying. The short assured tenant has little security of tenure. See appendix for an example of tenancy and notice (AT5) which must be served on the tenant prior to entering into the agreement stating that the agreement is a short assured tenancy.

The following are the conditions for the creation of a short assured tenancy:

- The tenancy fulfills the requirements of a valid assured tenancy.
- The landlord, before the creation of the tenancy, has served on the tenant a formal notice (AT5) stating that the proposed tenancy is to be a short assured. tenancy and giving various information set out in regulations.
- The tenancy is for a fixed period of not less than six-months (there is no maximum period).

One main difference between assured shorthold tenancies and short assured is that, if neither landlord nor tenant take any action to renew the tenancy at the end of the fixed period (6 months) then the tenancy will automatically renew for the same minimum fixed period (or one year if the fixed period was more than one year). This is known as tacit relocation.

Recovery of possession

A short assured tenant has no defence to a properly based possession action. The sheriff must grant an order for possession if he is satisfied that all of the following apply:

- The tenancy has reached its termination date.
- No tacit relocation is in action (i.e. a valid notice to quit of at least 40 days has been served by the landlord.
- No further contractual tenancy is in existence.
- The landlord has given at least two months notice to the tenant that he requires possession of the house. The notice can be served during the tenancy or after the termination date.

As with the English Assured shorthold, the landlord does not need to give any reason why he needs possession. In addition, because the short assured tenancy is a type of assured tenancy then recovery using the grounds for possession is the same as the assured tenancy. It can be seen that, apart from a number of minor differences, there are many similarities between the assured shorthold and the short assured tenancy.

Now read the main points from chapter eleven overleaf

****

Main points from Chapter 11

- Private sector tenancies in Scotland are regulated by the Housing (Scotland) Act 1988.
- Agreements of 1 year or more must be in writing. Agreements for less than 1 year can be verbal.
- The most common form of private sector tenancy is the short assured tenancy.
- There are many similarities between the short assured tenancy and the assured shorthold tenancy.

****

Chapter 12

Managing the Finances-Tax and Other Issues

This chapter explains some of the issues concerning allowances and taxation related to property that is being let out. It doesn't go into great depth, you would need an accountant to advise you on more complex matters, particularly if you are a landlord of multiple properties.

Allowable expenses

If you let out property you can deduct certain expenses and tax allowances from your rental income to work out your taxable profit and loss. If you have several UK residential lettings you pool the income and expenses together. Furnished holiday lettings and overseas lettings are worked out separately.

The expenses you can deduct from letting income (unless its under the rent a room scheme) include:

- Lettings agent's fees
- Legal fees for lettings of a year or less, or for renewing a lease for less than 50 years
- Accountants fees
- Buildings and contents insurance
- Interest on property loans (although this tax relief will now be reduced to 20% from 2017).
- Maintenance and repairs to the property (but not improvements
- Utility bills such as gas, electricity and water
- Rent, ground rent, service charges
- Council tax

- Services you pay for, such as cleaning and gardening
- Other direct costs of letting the property, such as phone calls, stationary and advertising

If your annual income for letting is less than £70,000 (before expenses) you include the total expenses on your tax return. If it is over £70,000 you need to provide a breakdown.

You can only claim expenses that are solely for running your property letting business. If the expense is only partly for running your business, or you live in the property yourself, then you may only be able to claim part of it.

Non-allowable expenses

When you work out profit, you can't deduct:

- 'Capital' costs, such as furniture or the property itself
- Personal expenses-costs that aren't to do with your lettings business
- Any loss you make when you sell the property

However, you may be able to claim some allowances instead. You should consult your accountant, or HMRC for further information about these allowances.

Furnished residential lettings

For furniture and equipment provided with a furnished residential letting (excluding furnished holiday lettings) you can claim a wear and tear allowance. The allowance is 10% of the net rent-that is rent received less any costs that you pay that a tenant would normally pay, for example council tax.

As an alternative to the wear and tear allowance, you can claim a 'renewals allowance'. This allowance covers the cost of replacing furniture or equipment including small items. Small items would include things such as cutlery.

To work it out, take the cost of the replacement item and deduct from it:

- The amount you sold the old one for (if anything)
- Anything extra you paid for a better one

Once you have chosen which of these allowances to claim for a property, you can't switch between them from year to year. You cannot claim capital allowances for equipment that is used in a dwelling house. Most residential accommodation is classed as a dwelling house.

Furnished holiday lettings

If you own a qualifying furnished holiday let in the UK, or European Union, you can claim capital allowances based on the cost of the furniture and equipment you provide with the property. Or you can claim a renewals allowance.

You cannot claim wear and tear. See capital allowances below. Also, see section on furnished holiday lettings below.

All letting properties

If you let out property you can deduct certain expenses and tax allowances from your rental income. Whatever letting it is, you can claim a capital allowance on the cost of things that you need for running your property letting business, such as a computer. You can also claim for equipment that isn't for the use of a single let property, like a new fire alarm system for a block of flats.

How much capital allowance can you claim?

There are different types of allowances. In some cases you can claim the full cost of an item as a deduction in the year that you buy it. In other cases you can claim all of your expenditure on various items in the year that you buy them. You may have to work out the allowance as the percentage of the value in a pool of expenditure. The allowance is deducted along with other allowances in calculating your profit.

If you use an item for anything other than your business you will have to work out the allowance for that item separately. You can only claim the amount that is for business use.

Which year do expenses apply to?

You have to allocate expenses to the year that they apply to-it doesn't matter when you actually pay for them. However, for capital allowance purposes, it does matter when the cost of the item is payable. You may have to allocate part of the expense to one year and part to another.

Losses

If your lettings business makes a loss, you can carry it forward` to a later year and offset it against future profits from the same business. The rules for holiday lettings are slightly different and you should check with HMRC for further clarification.

Working out tax payable

Work out 'net profit' as follows:

- Add up all of your rental income
- Add up all of you allowable expenses
- Take allowable expenses away from income

If you have more than one residential letting, group all the income and expenses together.

To arrive at your taxable profit, deduct any allowable expenses away from your net profit. If you let furnished property, you can deduct either of the following:

- A wear and tear allowance-based on a percentage of your rent, as mentioned above
- A renewals allowance, as mentioned above

As stated, you can't claim both allowances.

Reporting profits to HMRC

If your profit is less than £2,500 and you are employed or paying tax on a pension then your tax code can be adjusted to collect tax on your property income each year.

If your profit is £2,500 or more or you are not on PAYE

In this case you will need to fill in a self- assessment tax return. If your total income from property is more than £70,000 in one tax year (based on 2015-2016) you must declare it on your tax return. You must also show your expenses separately. If it's below £70,000 you can group it as a single total on your return.

When you fill in your return put the rent and expenses in the year that they relate to-it doesn't matter when you receive them.

How much tax is paid?

Your taxable profit form property letting is added to your income. Tax will be charged at the appropriate rate.

If you let property jointly, with someone else, when you fill in your tax returns you should each show your respective shares.

Capital gains tax

When you come to sell the property, you will be liable for CGT, but only on the gains that you have made. You have a personal CGT allowance of £11,100 (2015-16) a year. If the property is held in joint names, with a spouse or partner you can add your allowances together.

Any net taxable gain in the year is added to your total income from other sources in the year to determine the tax band.

If the property was formerly your main residence, you are exempt from CGT if you sell within three years of it becoming a rental property. Where a gain is made on disposal of a property that has been a main residence at some point, but has also been specifically let as residential accommodation, then a further special relief is available. This exempts a gain of up to £40,000.

If the property was never your main residence, you are liable for full CGT for the first three years. After that, the proportion of the tax charged is tapered for the next seven years. There is a reduction of 5% each year after three years increasing by 5% each year to a maximum of 40% of the gain, after 10 years. This equates to effective tax rates for higher rate payers of 24% and 13.8% for lower rate payers.

Tax on furnished holiday lettings

If you let out a furnished holiday home in the UK or European Economic Area (EEA) you may be entitled to certain tax advantages. However, your property must meet some rules to qualify.

Rules for furnished holiday lettings

To make sure that a property qualifies as a holiday letting, it must be:

- In the UK or EEA
- Furnished
- Available for commercial letting to the public, as holiday accommodation, for at least 210 days a year

- Commercially let as holiday accommodation for at least 105 days a year-the rent must be charged at market rent and not at cheap rates to friends or family
- A short term letting of no more than 31 days

Tax advantage of furnished holiday lettings

The tax advantages if your property qualifies as a holiday home are:

- You can claim capital allowances
- You get the benefit of some favorable capital gains tax rules when you sell, or otherwise dispose of the property.

Working out taxable profit

The profit on furnished holiday lettings is worked out in the same way as other lettings income. The only difference is that you can claim capital allowances rather than wear and tear allowances that other rental businesses receive. Examples of expenses that qualify for capital allowances include the cost of furnishings and furniture and equipment such as refrigerators and washing machines.

If you make a loss

You can carry a loss forward and offset it against future lettings profits. If you have a UK holiday home the losses can only reduce the future holiday let profits of the UK home, likewise with a EEA holiday home. You cannot use a holiday let loss to reduce your other income.

If you sell or 'otherwise dispose' of the property

You may be able to take advantages of capital gains tax relief's, such as 'business asset roll-over relief'. For example, if you reinvest the sale proceeds within three years in certain other business assets, you may be able to defer payment of Capital Gains Tax until you dispose of those new assets.

More information can be obtained from HMRC.

You should declare your income from furnished holiday lets on your UK self-assessment tax return.

Inheritance tax

When you die, any buy to let properties you own will be included in your estate. If your whole estate is worth more than £325,000-or £650,000 for married couples, then you will be liable for inheritance tax. Above the thresholds the tax charged is 40%.

Keeping records

For all property lettings it is very important to keep records of all income and expenditure and associated receipts. As with all business, accurate record keeping is vital.

As a guide, your records should include:

- All the rent you should receive and dates when you let out your property
- Any income from services provided to tenants
- Your business expenses
- Rent books, receipt, invoices and bank statements

Now read the main points from Chapter 12 overleaf

****

Main points from Chapter 12

- If you let out property you can deduct certain expenses and tax allowances from your rental income

- If you own a qualifying furnished holiday let in the UK, or European Union, you can claim capital allowances based on the cost of the furniture and equipment you provide with the property

- If you let out property you can deduct certain expenses and tax allowances from your rental income

- If your lettings business makes a loss, you can carry it forward

- When you come to sell the property, you will be liable for CGT, but only on the gains that you have made

- For all property lettings it is very important to keep records of all income and expenditure and associated receipts

****

Useful websites

The Buying Process

The Local Government Association
www.lga.gov.uk
Confederation of Scottish Local Authorities
www.cosla.gov.uk
Greater London Authority
www.london.gov.uk
The Environment Agency
www.environment-agency.gov.uk
www.homecheckuk.com

House Prices

Halifax www.halifax.co.uk
Nationwide www.nationwide.co.uk
Land Registry www.landreg.gov.uk
www.zoopla.co.uk
www.ourproperty.co.uk
www.upmystreet.com

Property search sites

www.hometrack.co.uk
www.rightmove.co.uk
www.zoopla.co.uk
www.fish4.co.uk
www.findaproperty.com
www.thisislondon.co.uk

The buying and selling process

The Law Society www.lawsoc.org.uk
The Council of Mortgage Lenders www.cml.org.uk

HM Customs and Revenue www.hmrc.gov

Scotland

Law Society of Scotland www.scotlaw.org.uk

Leasehold/freehold

Lease www.lease-advice.org
Association of Residential Managing Agents
www.arma.org.uk

Mortgage search sites/brokers

Money facts www.moneyfacts.co.uk
www.moneysupermarket.co.uk
www.moneynet.co.uk

New homes

NHBC www.nhbc.co.uk

Renting and Letting

Association of Residential Letting Agencies (ARLA)
ARLA Administration
Maple House
53-55 Woodside Road
Amersham
Bucks
HP6 6AA
Tel: 01923 896555
Website: www.arla.co.uk
Email: info@arla.co.uk

Specialist rental property sites

www.zoopla.co.uk

www.rightmove.co.uk

Auctions

www.propwatch.com

www.primelocation.com

www.bbc.co.uk/homes/property/buying_auction

www.propertyauctions.com

www.netguide.co.uk/Buying_A_House_At_Auction

A SUMMARY OF IMPORTANT TERMS

FREEHOLDER: Someone who owns their property outright.

LEASEHOLDER: Someone who has been granted permission to live on someone else's land for a fixed term.

TENANCY: One form of lease, the most common types of which are fixed-term or periodic.

LANDLORD: A person who owns the property in which the tenant lives.

LICENCE: A licence is an agreement entered into whereby the landlord is merely giving you permission to occupy his/her property for a limited period of time.

TRESPASSER: Someone who has no right through an agreement to live in a property.

PROTECTED TENANT: In the main, subject to certain exclusions, someone whose tenancy began before 15th January 1989.

ASSURED TENANT: In the main, subject to certain exclusions, someone whose tenancy began after 15th January 1989.

NOTICE TO QUIT: A legal document giving the protected tenant twenty eight days notice that the landlord intends to apply for possession of the property to the County Court.

GROUND FOR POSSESSION: One of the stated reasons for which the landlord can apply for possession of the property.

MANDATORY GROUND: Where the judge must give possession of the property.

DISCRETIONARY GROUND: Where the judge may or may not give possession, depending on his own opinion.

STUDENT LETTING: A tenancy granted by a specified educational institution.

HOLIDAY LETTING: A dwelling used for holiday purposes only.

ASSURED SHORTHOLD TENANCY: A fixed-term post-1989 tenancy.

PAYMENT OF RENT: Where you pay a regular sum of money in return for permission to occupy a property or land for a specified period of time.

FAIR RENT: A rent set by the Rent Officer every two years for most pre-1989 tenancies and is lower than a market rent.

MARKET RENT: A rent deemed to be comparable with other non-fair rents in the area.

RENT ASSESSMENT COMMITTEE: A committee set up to review rents set by either the Rent Officer or the landlord.

PREMIUM: A sum of money charged for permission to live in a property.

DEPOSIT: A sum of money held against the possibility of damage to property.

QUIET ENJOYMENT: The right to live peacefully in your own home.

REPAIRS: Work required to keep a property in good order.

IMPROVEMENTS: Alterations to a property.

LEGAL AID: Help with your legal costs, which is dependent on income.

HOUSING BENEFIT: Financial help with rent, which is dependent on income.

HOUSING ADVICE CENTRE: A center which exists to give advice on housing-related matters and which is usually local authority-funded.

LAW CENTRE: A center, which exists for the purpose of assisting the public with legal advice.

****

Index

****

Appendix 1

Sample Assured Shorthold Tenancy Agreement (England and Wales)

Sample Section 21 Notice Requiring possession

Sample Notices Scotland

Sample Landlords Inventory

ASSURED SHORTHOLD TENANCY AGREEMENT ENGLAND AND WALES

This Tenancy Agreement is between

Name and address of Landlord-

-AND

Name of tenant:

nt"

(in the case of Joint Tenants the term "Tenant" applies to each of them and the names of all Joint Tenants should be written above. Each Tenant individually has the full responsibilities and rights set out in this Agreement)

Address-in respect of:

("the Premises")

Description of Premises

-Which comprises of:

Term-The Tenancy is granted for a fixed term of [6] months

Date of start of tenancy-The Tenancy begins on:

("The Commencement Date") and is an assured shorthold monthly tenancy, the terms of which are set out in this Agreement.

Overcrowding-The Tenant agrees not to allow any person other than the Tenant to reside at the Premises.

Payment of Deposit-The Tenant agrees to pay on signing the Agreement a deposit of £ which will be returnable in full providing that the Landlord may deduct from such sums: The reasonable costs of any necessary repairs to the premises, building or common parts, or the replacement of any or all of the contents where such repair or replacement is due to any act or omission of the Tenant or family or visitors of the Tenant, such sums as are outstanding on leaving the Premises in respect of arrears or other charges including Court costs or other fees.

The deposit will be protected by The Deposit Protection Service (The DPS) in accordance with the Terms and Conditions of The DPS. The Terms and Conditions and ADR Rules governing the protection of the deposit including the repayment process can be found at www.depositprotection.com

Payment for the premises-
Rent: The rent for the premises is:

Service Charge:
Total:

In this Agreement the term "Rent" refers to the net rent and service charge set out above or as varied from time to time in accordance with this Agreement. The payment of monthly Rent is due in advance on the first Saturday of each month.

The service charge is in respect of the landlord providing the services listed in Schedule 1 to this Agreement for which the Tenant shall pay a service charge to be included in the rent. The service charge may be varied by the landlord in accordance with the terms set out in Schedule 1 to this Agreement.

I/We have read, understood and accept the terms and conditions contained within this agreement which include the standard terms and conditions attached.

Signed by the Tenant

.... Dated:

Signed on behalf of the landlord
.... Dated:

If the Tenant feels that the landlord has broken this Agreement or not performed any obligation contained in it, he/she should first complain to the landlord in writing giving details of the breach or non-performance.

Terms and Conditions

1. It is agreed that:
Changes in Rent-1.1-The landlord may increase or decrease the Rent by giving the Tenant not less than 4 weeks notice in writing of the increase or decrease. The notice shall specify the Rent proposed. The first increase or decrease shall be on the first day of   following the Commencement Date of this Agreement. Subsequent increases or decreases in the Rent shall take effect on the first day of   in each subsequent year. The revised Rent shall be the amount specified in the notice of increase unless the Tenant exercises his/her right to refer the notice to a Rent Assessment Committee to have a market rent determined in which case the maximum Rent payable for one year after the date specified in the notice shall be the Rent so determined.

Altering the Agreement-1.2-With the exception of any changes in Rent, this Agreement may only be altered by the agreement in writing of both the Tenant and the landlord.

2. The landlord agrees:

Possession-2.1-To give the Tenant possession of the Premises at the commencement of the Tenancy.

Tenant's Right to Occupy-2.2-Not to interrupt or interfere with the Tenant's right peacefully to occupy the Premises except where:

(i) access is required to inspect the condition of the Premises or to carry out repairs or other works to the Premises or adjoining property; or

(ii) a court has given the Association possession by ending the Tenancy.

Repair of Structure and Exterior-2.3-To keep in good repair the structure and exterior of the Premises including:

(i) drains, gutters and external pipes;

(ii) the roof;

(iii) outside wall, outside doors, windowsills, window catches, sash cords and window frames including necessary external painting and decorating;

(iv) internal walls, floors and ceilings, doors and door frames, door hinges and skirting boards but not including internal painting and decoration;

(v) plasterwork;

(vi) chimneys, chimney stacks and flues but not including sweeping;

(vii) pathways, steps or other means of access;

(viii) integral garages and stores;

(ix) boundary walls and fences.

Repair of Installations-2.4-To keep in good repair and working order any installations provided by the landlord for space heating, water heating and sanitation and for the supply of water, gas and electricity including:

(i) basins, sinks, baths, toilets, flushing systems and waste pipes;

(ii) electric wiring including sockets and switches, gas pipes and water pipes;

(iii) water heaters, fireplaces, fitted fires and central heating installations

Repair of Common Parts-2.5-To take reasonable care to keep the common entrances, halls, stairways, lifts, passageways, rubbish chutes and any other common parts, including their lighting, in reasonable repair and fit for use by the Tenant and other occupiers and visitors to the Premises.

External & Internal Decorations-2.6-To keep the exterior and interior of the Premises and any common parts in a good state of decoration and normally to decorate these areas once every 5 years.

3. The Tenant agrees:

Possession-3.1-To take possession of the Premises at the commencement of the Tenancy and not to part with possession of the Premises or sub-let the whole or part of it.

Rent-3.2-To pay the Rent monthly and in advance. The first payment shall be made on the signing of the Agreement in respect of the period from the Commencement Date to the first Saturday of the following month.

Use of Premises-3.3-To use the Premises for residential purposes as the Tenant's only or principal home and not to operate a business at the Premises without the written consent of the landlord.

Nuisance and Racial and other Harassment-3.4-Not to behave or allow members of his/her household or any other person visiting the Premises with the Tenant's permission to behave in a manner nor do anything which is likely to be a nuisance to the tenants, owners or lessees of any of the other properties or other persons lawfully visiting the property. In particular, not to cause any interference, nuisance or annoyance through noise, anti-social behaviour or threats of or actual violence or any damage to property belonging to the said persons. This Clause also applies to any conduct or activity which amounts to harassment including: abuse and intimidation, creating unacceptable levels of noise or causing intentional damage or any other persistent behaviour which causes offence, discomfort or inconvenience on the grounds of colour, race religion, sex, sexual orientation and disability.

Noise-3.5-Not to play or allow to be played any radio, television, audio equipment or musical instrument so loudly that it causes a nuisance or annoyance to neighbours or can be heard outside the Premises.

Domestic Violence-3.6-Not to use or threaten violence against any other person living in the Premises such that they are forced to leave by reason of the Tenant's violence or fear of such violence.

Pets-3.7-To keep under control any animals at the Premises and to obtain the written consent of the landlord before keeping a dog or any other animal.

Car Repairs-3.8-That no car servicing or car repairs shall be carried out in the roads or accessway or parking spaces or in the forecourt or approaches to the Premises, such as to be a nuisance or annoyance to neighbours.

Paraffin-3.9-Not to use any paraffin or bottled gas heating, lighting or cooking appliances on the Premises nor any appliances which discharge the products of combustion into the interior of the Premises.

Vehicles-3.10-That no commercial vehicle, caravan, boat, or lorry shall be parked in the accessway or parking spaces (regardless of whether this forms part of the Premises) or in the forecourt or approaches to the Premises or the adjoining premises.

Keeping premises clean-3.11-To keep the interior of the Premises in a clean condition. The Tenant agrees to return the property in the same decorative order as at the start of the tenancy taking into account fair wear and tear.

Damage-3.12-To make good any damage caused wilfully or by neglect or carelessness on the part of the Tenant or any member of the Tenant's household or visitor to the Premises including the replacement of any broken glass in windows and repair or replacement of any damaged fittings and installations. If the Tenant fails to make good any damage for which he/she is responsible the landlord may enter the Premises and carry out the work in default and the cost of this work shall be recoverable by the Association from the Tenant.

Reporting Disrepair-3.13-To report to the landlord any disrepair or defect for which the landlord is responsible in the structure or exterior of the Premises or in any installation therein or in the common parts.

Access-3.14-To allow the landlords employees or contractors acting on behalf of the landlord access at all reasonable hours of the daytime to inspect the condition of the Premises or to carry out repairs or other works to the Premises or adjoining property. The landlord will normally give at least 24 hours' notice, but immediate access may be required and shall be given in an emergency.

Assignment-3.15-Not to assign the Tenancy.

Sub-Tenants-3.16-Not to sub-let the whole or part of the Premises.

Ending the Tenancy-3.17-To give the landlord at least [4] weeks notice in writing when the Tenant wishes to end the Tenancy.

Moving Out-3.18-To give the landlord vacant possession and return the keys of the Premises at the end of the Tenancy and to remove all personal possessions and rubbish and leave the Premises and the landlords furniture and fixtures in good lettable condition and repair. The landlord accepts no responsibility for anything left at the Premises by the Tenant at the end of the Tenancy.

4. The Tenant has the following rights:

Right to Occupy-4.1-The Tenant has the right to occupy the Premises without interruption or interference from the landlord for the duration of this Tenancy (except for the obligation contained in this Agreement to give access to the landlords employees or contractors) so long as the Tenant complies with the terms of this Agreement and has proper respect for the rights of other tenants and neighbours.

Security of Tenure-4.2-The Tenant has security of tenure as an assured tenant so long as he/she occupies the Premises as his/her only or principal home. Before the expiry of the fixed term the landlord can only end the Tenancy by obtaining a court order for possession of the Premises on one of the grounds listed in Schedule 2 of the Housing Act 1988. The landlord will only use the following grounds to obtain an order for possession

(i) --The tenant has not paid rent which is due; (Ground 10)

(ii) The Tenant has broken, or failed to perform, any of the conditions of this Tenancy; (Ground 12)

(iii) The Tenant or anyone living in the premises has caused damage to, or failed to look after the premises, the building, any of the common parts; (Ground 13)

(iv) The Tenant or anyone living in the premises has caused serious or persistent nuisance or annoyance to neighbours, or has been responsible for any act of harassment on the grounds of race, colour, religion, sex, sexual orientation, or disability, or has been convicted of using the property for immoral or illegal purposes; (Ground 14) or because of domestic violence (Ground 14A)

(v) Where the tenancy has devolved under the will or intestacy of the Tenant

(vi) Suitable alternative accommodation is available to the Tenant

Notice Periods for ending Assured Tenancy-4.3-Before the expiry of the fixed term the landlord agrees that it will not give less than four weeks notice in writing of its intention to seek a possession order except where it is seeking possession on Ground 14 or Ground 14A (whether or not combined with other Grounds) where it shall give such period of notice that it shall decide and that is not less than the statutory minimum notice period

Expiry of Tenancy-4.4-The landlord can only end the Tenancy by giving the Tenant at least two months notice that it requires possession of the Premises and by obtaining a court order for possession. The court will make an order for possession if it is satisfied that the proper notice has been given.

Cessation of Assured Tenancy-4.5-If the Tenancy ceases to be an assured tenancy the landlord may end the Tenancy by giving four weeks' notice in writing which shall be validly served on the Tenant if posted or delivered to the Premises.

As amended by Section 98 Housing Act 1996)
Section 21 (a or b depending on when served)
Assured Shorthold Tenancy
Notice Requiring Possession

TO:-

OF:-Address:

FROM:- (Landlord)

OF:-

HEREBY GIVE YOU NOTICE THAT POSSESSION IS REQUIRED

by virtue of section 21 Housing Act 1988 of the premises

-Address:

Which you hold as tenant after the

Signed On behalf of (Landlord):

....

Date:

Print Name:

Note

1. If the tenant does not leave the dwelling the landlord must get an order for possession from the court before the tenant can be legally evicted. The landlord cannot apply for such an order before the notice has run out.

2. A tenant who does not know if he has any rights to remain in possession after a notice runs out or is otherwise unsure of his rights can obtain advice from a solicitor. Help with all or part of the cost of legal advice and assistance may be available under the legal aid scheme. He should also be able to obtain information from a Citizens Advice Bureau, a Housing Aid Centre or a Rent Officer

****

SCOTLAND

LANDLORDS NOTICE TO TERMINATE SHORT ASSURED TENANCY

FROM:

LANDLORDS NAME AND
ADDRESS____

____

____

____

TO:
TENANT____

____

____

____

DATE________________________

PROPERTY____

____

____

____

The above landlord hereby gives formal notice to the above tenant under section 33 of the Housing (Scotland) Act 1988 of their intention to bring the tenants tenancy to an end and recover possession of the above property currently occupied by the tenant.

In terms of section 33 of the aforementioned Act the tenant must receive at least two months notice of the landlords intention to recover possession. Please therefore take note that you are required to vacate the premises no later than________________________________

Note: This Notice to terminate and the Notice to Quit overleaf should both be completed and sent to the tenant at least two months before the end of the tenancy.

SCOTLAND

SHORT ASSURED TENANCY NOTICE TO QUIT

NOTI CE OF REMOVAL UNDER SECTION 37 OF THE SHERIFF COURTS (SCOTLAND) ACT 1907

FROM:
LANDLORD____
____
____

TO:
TENANT____
____
____

DATE:__________________________

PROPERTY____
____

The above landlords hereby give notice to the above tenant that the tenant is required to remove from the property at the______ day of________ in terms of the lease between landlord and tenant.

The undernoted schedule which is incorporated herein complied with the Assured Tenancies (Notice to Quit Information) (Scotland) Regulations 1988.

Schedule

1. Even after the Notice to Quit has run out, before the tenant can be lawfully evicted, the landlord must get an order or possession from the court.

2. If the landlord issues a Notice to Quit but does not seek to gain possession of the property in question the contractual assured tenancy which has been terminated will be replaced by a Statutory Assured Tenancy. In such circumstances the landlord may propose new terms for the tenancy and may seek an adjustment to the rent at annual intervals thereafter.

3. If a tenant does not know what type of tenancy he has or is otherwise unsure of his rights he can obtain advice from a solicitor. Help with all or part of the cost of legal advice and assistance can be available under the legal aid legislation. A tenant can also seek help from a Citizens Advice Bureau or Housing Advisory centre.

ENGLAND AND WALES AND SCOTLAND HOUSEHOLD INVENTORY

Re: (The Property)________________________________

Living room				
No	Item	Condition	In	Out
1	Armchair	Fair		(condition when leaving)
Etc Etc				
Kitchen				
Bathroom				

Hall				
Bedroom (1-2-3)				
Garden				
Other				